Innovation
In Hard Times

Also by Ian Goult

Secret Location
A witness to the Birth of Radar
and its Post-war Influence

Vapour Trails - a novella

Ten Short Stories - Kindle

Trauma Made Redundant -
under the pseudonym of Ewen Gould

Innovation
In Hard Times

Ian Goult

First published: 2015

Issue 3 2016

ISBN 9781516839810

Published by: Ian Goult

CONTENTS

Acknowledgements
Preface
Introduction

Chapter 1   Typical local entrepreneurs.
Chapter 2   The ultimate innovator
Chapter 3   Science, innovation and attitudes
          Article by Professor Malcolm Baird
Chapter 4   Early history of a great innovation
Chapter 5   Innovation through IC
Chapter 6   People Capital
Chapter 7   Early enablers of the digital era
Chapter 8   Analogue to Digital
An optional chapter - "digital" in simple terms
Chapter 9   Clerk Maxwell - *his importance*
Chapter 10   Links to the "www" innovation
Chapter 11   Creators of the digital era
Chapter 12   The Silicon Chip
Chapter 13   Knowledge Management
Chapter 14   Life before television!
Conclusion

Acknowledgements

The author wishes to acknowledge with gratitude the following: Professor Malcolm Baird for his continuous advice and encouragement throughout the preparation of this book and especially for his Article on Science, Innovation and Attitudes, and many other additional comments, to Professor Keith Moffatt for permission to publish his delightful poem Genius o' Glenlair, together with corrections and advice relating to James Clerk Maxwell from the James Clerk Maxwell Foundation.

The Port of Felixstowe kindly permitted the use of data from their history of 100 YEARS A WORKING PORT, in particular its innovative development into one of the world's largest container Ports

Thanks are also due to my daughters, Alison for suggesting I wrote the book in the first place, and keeping me at it, and to Jane for her excellent advice on The Management of Knowledge.

Walton Mill was sketched thanks to Nan Drew, adding the missing sails!

PREFACE

Although there are many books relating to the depression and unemployment of the inter-war years, around 80% of the population were not unemployed. It is of this section of the community that persevered with positive attitudes and established new ventures some of which changed the way we live, as witnessed by the author, both directly and from personal contacts during this period that is the main scope of this book. It also covers the immediate post-world-war II period. In both periods there were remarkable examples witnessed of intellectual and people capital when financial capital was in short supply or not available at all.

The author has spent a lifetime in industrial research and development both in the UK, and the USA witnessing innovation, entrepreneurial enterprises and the use of Intelligence Capital (IC), its importance during economic recession, in particular during interwar and immediate post-war years, together with Knowledge Management as witnessed before it was a tool of today's project managers. The background of some of these events was to lead to the fascinating lives of and work of others in an earlier period such as the great mathematicians, physicists and Logicians of thet19th century who were to have an impact on the post-world-war II technical advances.

The Innovative and entrepreneurial activities in small communities across the country, each on its own of little significance, but taken across the country as a whole of considerable significance, was witnessed as an example in the author's home town with the development of three of the largest hotels on the sea front of Felixstowe following the first world war and at it apogee at the time of the great depression of 1929.

An example of the most innovative yet understated example of personal innovation carried out during a period of industrial decline, coming to fruition and success at the very time of the economic collapse of 1929 – 1932; carried out against all the odds with virtually no financial backing; yet taken for granted now, was surely the work of John Logie Baird; an example of intelligence capital overriding financial capital. There was no financial capital until Baird Television Ltd was created, broadcasting the world's first television programmes. This is followed by observations on science, innovation and attitudes by Baird's son Professor Malcolm Baird.

Post-World-War 11, during the lean years there is another, but very different example of innovation

– the establishment of one of the largest container ports in the world from a virtually derelict and silted up small dock basin; carried through with no financial backing, innovating procedures that were to become standard world-wide.

During the austerity of the post-war period the UK, ahead of the world in computer technology whilst struggling to overcome the run down state of industry, the work of the early pioneers of computer development such as Turing, Flowers and "FC" Williams is described together with the fundamental work of the great mathematicians of the nineteenth century, Boole, De Morgan, Babbage, and Clerk Maxwell, with their link to the computer and internet era via Hertz and Marconi.

Finally the impact of knowledge management is discussed before its formalisation by today's project managers.

Introduction

The general perception of the 20s and 30s has tended to be critical of the governance of that period; however the crash of 1929 – 1932 was global and Great Britain suffered less than many other countries. Thereafter there was a surprisingly good working relationship between the conservative prime minister Stanley Baldwin and the labour leader Ramsay McDonald (though suspended from the party as a result) during the national government, doing their best in a difficult economic climate. Only subsequently has it been acknowledged that there was little hope of reviving the traditional industries of the past. Hope lay in looking to the future, as at present.

Examples of entrepreneurial innovation in times of economic downturn are the purpose of this book. Not only the great innovators but also in the smaller communities, towns and villages across the country each on its own of little significance, but of considerable significance when taken across the country as a whole; the substance of chapter 1; as important to the main economy as the large industrial complexes.

It is tempting to think in terms of a typical small town; but there is no such thing. Each small town or village is, or was, unique in the interwar years prior to the introduction of supermarkets.   But they all had a community spirit. - a spirit which is less apparent today although it does lie dormant below the surface; surfacing in times of local disaster as witnessed during the floods in the first months of 2014.

The small town chosen was the one in which the author grew up.

In the years of austerity after World war 11 there was a very different example of innovation – the establishment of one of the largest container ports in the world from a virtually derelict and silted up small dock basin purchased for £50,000. This was carried through with no financial backing using innovative procedures that were to become standard world-wide. This feat is described in part 2.

Following world-war II the country was financially exhausted. The euphoria of VE Day May 8th 1945 soon wore off.

In contrast to West Germany which pulling itself together and rebuilding itself by concerted personal and national determination, with generous assistance from the United States through marshal aid, and France which had built up its Industrial structure by cooperation with Germany following German occupation in 1940, the UK was in a state of economic ruin continuing to experience relative economic decline for years to follow. Far from benefitting from marshal aid, it was in debt to the United

States, primarily for the lease-lend and purchasing arrangements of the war.

West Germany had by the end of the 1950s doubled production from its pre-war levels. By the 1950s, the Italian economy was growing rapidly. France, modernising its industry, was becoming the dominant force in Europe.

The UK was bedevilled by political dogma, discouraging enterprise, the modernisation of industry struggling with old and worn out machine tools, preventing individual entrepreneurial activities and innovation until the arrival of the Morris Mini and the swinging sixties.

Malcolm Baird comments:

"From my vantage point, I remember very tough times in the UK in the 1940s and early 1950s including rationing, taxation, foreign currency restrictions etc. However, unemployment was less than 3%. The emphasis was on manufacturing for export, while home consumption was heavily restricted. Purchase tax on cars, radios and TV sets was very high and hire purchase did not come on the scene until late 1950s. Many of my fellow students at Glasgow University (class of 1957) emigrated - Engineers, scientists, teachers, nurses, etc.

"Although employment was high, modernisation was seen as a threat to employment. The film comedy "I'm All Right, Jack" gives us a flavour of the attitudes. In spite of the post war economic constraints, UK put a lot of money into house construction. It is a pity that little money was invested in modern manufacturing; this could have been encouraged by tax incentives"

Bucking this post war trend was a remarkable example of innovation carried out with only people and intelligence capital – the establishment of one of the largest container ports in the world from a virtually derelict and silted up small dock basin purchased for £50,000, carried through with no financial backing, innovating procedures that were to become standard world-wide.

This austerity period ended in the "Swinging Sixties" with the beginning of a new era – an era that was the based on the work of arguably two of the greatest physicists and mathematicians prior to Einstein – James Clerk Maxwell, with his ground breaking equations relating to the transmission of electromagnetic waves, and George Boole, logician, formalising Boolean algebra – the engines of the World Wide Web. Their work and life, together with that of contemporaries Augustus De Morgan and Charles Babbage are linked to Alan Turing, Thomas Flowers and "FC" Williams via Heinrich Hertz and Guglielmo Marconi to establish the UK's immediate post-war lead in computer technology, its demise due to the paucity of intellectual capital during the "recovery" of the swinging sixties and end of austerity. The beginning of the new digital era was initiated elsewhere.

There is an optional chapter offering a simple explanation of the term digital in relation to digital data.

CHAPTER I

Minor Entrepreneurs in small communities

Malcolm Baird Comments:

"This is an interesting family history with pictures, taking us up to 1916. The scale was very small and only modest amounts of capital were involved; it is not very clear where this came from – personal savings, or family money or bank loans? Taxation was virtually non-existent but so were government support schemes!

The rates of growth and change were slow compared to the 20th century.

It is also interesting to comment on the sort of people who set up the businesses. NOT the aristocracy and not the high academics, but small landowners and people engaged in "trade" or mechanical work."

Background:

Walton Mill Sketch by Nan Drew (adding sails)

It was in Felixstowe, a small seaside resort prior to the building of the great container port for which it is known today, that the author witnessed the interwar years; although not with great perception until the thirties. Prior to that it was the author's grandfather and later his mother, active in the community during the earlier period and it is their story that plays a large part of this witness of the growth of a small business in a small town during these years.

It was from the Bloomfield's of Walton that was to lead to this typical small town entrepreneurial activity of the inter war years.

Walton mill, which still stands in the village of Walton in Suffolk, less the sails, was run by the author's great grandfather, John Bloomfield; a tower mill, it ground corn, to be shipped to London by his barge from Walton creek, later to be the sight for the Port of Felixstowe, one of the largest in the world.

John Bloomfield (born 1834), himself one of nine children, married to Rachel Jane Wharton from the nearby village of Trimley, had 17 children of which 12 survived. Alice, pictured on the far right of the back row in the following photograph, married William Dawson. It was the Dawson's with their daughters that are the examples of the positive entrepreneurs in Felixstowe during the recession of the 1920s.

The twelve surviving children of John and Rachel
Bloomfield (centre). It was Alice (at the right of
the picture) who was also the guiding spirit to
turn a group of boarding houses into a group of
three of the largest hotels on the sea front at

Felixstowe. This was achieved despite suffering from chronic bronchitis, possibly the result of the flu epidemic following the war in 1918, which wiped out more people world-wide than the war itself

A witness to local entrepreneurs; 1918 - 1939

Alice Dawson and William Dawson

William Dawson was a tenant dairy farmer. Alice Dawson (nee Bloomfield) ran a dairy complete with milk maids. A horse and cart made a local house to house delivery. There were no bottles or cartons. The milk was contained in a large urn. The house-holder would come out with a jug; a measuring cup was dipped into the urn and the milk poured into the jug. In addition Alice ran several boarding houses on Felixstowe sea front.

William Dawson had four daughters The eldest, Evelyn married Frank Goult, who, following demobilisation, joined his father-in-law to set up a Garage and local bus service.

The car standing outside the early corrugated iron shed of Dawson and Goult was probably a Model

T Ford, the first of the Ford Company's mass production cars. Cars at this time were comparatively rare and still a bit of a novelty.

To start the bus and charabanc service second hand buses were purchased to be fully overhauled in the workshop, including engine and body rebuild as necessary.

As the business grew so did the premises. Alongside were 50 private lock-up garages for the safe keeping of the new car owners who had no garages attached to their homes and were reluctant to leave their precious acquisitions in the road.

William Dawson appreciating the increasing popularity of seaside holidays started to buy boarding houses one by one until he had control of the whole block which he converted into his first hotel – the Marlborough, later purchasing the Felix Court, and renting the Chatsworth.

Carnival 1929, the Marlborough Hotel

The Chatsworth & Felix Court Hotels circa 1939
The Felix Court extension was added in 1929/30,
at the height of the recession!

The farm and hotels must have been running concurrently, because one of the author's earliest memory was of plucking chickens in the farmyard. I can still sense the cold slimy feel of those dead chickens. Another more exciting and interesting memory was seeing the kitchen sink at the Chatsworth Hotel full of newly hatched baby chicks!! At a somewhat later age my cousin, John, and I would climb up to the roof of the Felix Court and from behind the tiled ridge dazzle the walkers on the promenade with mirrors.

The hotels prospered. Foreign travel was not then commonplace, other than expensive cruises for the upper echelons of society. A seaside holiday was typical. The Felixstowe hotels were holiday hotels

Originally bathrooms and toilets were separate. However all rooms had a basins and before breakfast a fleet of chambermaids would carry hot water jugs to each room. "Slops" were collected during breakfast. There were however some old fashioned observances that are not seen today. Every one of the 130 residents could have a clean linen napkin in his place for every meal. A jug of fresh water with glasses was placed on every table for lunch and dinner.

One week full board of breakfast, lunch, tea and dinner cost four to six pounds per week per person!

Staff, waitresses, chambermaids, porters, cooks (not chefs, they were too expensive) were hired from the local villages; some would sleep in. Wages would be typically two pounds a week with one day off.

The hotels, garage and bus service kept the family so busy there was never time for holidays; although it could be argued that living by the sea was all holiday - for the children.

William Dawson had been active in local affairs, becoming a local councillor, anxious to improve the attractions of the town, promoting the re-building of the old Spa Pavilion with its associated bandstand and gardens. After his death his daughter, Evelyn, followed in his footsteps to become the first lady councillor, and later the first Lady 'Chairman,' devoting herself to the further improvement of the resort promoting improvements to the Spa Garden and rebuilding the Pier Pavilion

During this inter war period the resort reached the apex of success at the peak of the Industrial recession!

CHAPTER 2

The Ultimate Innovator

John Logie Baird, 1888-1946

John Logie Baird was the undisputed inventor of television. This he achieved against all the odds.

Baird knew that the transmission of vision was possible and nothing was going to deflect him from achieving it He had the basic knowledge of the laws of physics, learned in his first year at the Royal technical college, Glasgow (now the University of Strathclyde) and he knew that all the elements were there for the realisation of television   However unlike researchers at industrial or academic laboratories he had no equipment or facilities to pursue his investigations, but pursue them he would.

In the early 1920's Baird moved to from London to Hastings for the benefit of his poor health following some somewhat bizarre activities such as developing the Baird under-sock for keeping the feet warm. This was a modest success, but he had embarked on a much less successful venture in Trinidad from which he returned in poor health with most of his capital gone.

It was whilst walking along the cliffs at Hastings that he resolved to pursue his earlier experiments for the transmission of moving images. These had been hampered by the lack of sensitivity of the selenium photo-electric cells needed to produce an electric current when exposed to light.   Baird realised that the development of the thermionic valve by Ambrose Fleming (the diode in 1904) and amplifying triode derivative by Lee De Forest (1907) would solve this problem.

The room at his lodgings in Hasting would become his laboratory. The equipment needed would have to be developed by whatever was available from his limited resources.

Briefly, in the early days, prior to development of the cathode ray tube Baird scanned the image by a fast rotating disk with a spiral of holes – rotating many times faster than the blink of an eye. The light reflected from the image through the consecutive spiral of holes on the disk focussed on the selenium photo-electric cell converting the light into a fluctuating electric current. The current was greatly amplified and the variations transmitted. An inverse arrangement at the receiver would project the image onto a ground glass screen. This is an over-simplification. Problems related to timing and picture resolution needed further sophistication.

Starting with no lab facilities Baird set about creating them: a tin biscuit box, a cardboard hat box, sealing wax, glue, an electric motor taken from an electric fan, and a and focusing lens from a torch, supplemented by the acquisition of batteries, lamps and of course selenium cells and thermionic valves. The first discs were made from cardboard with the spiral of holes cut out with scissors. After a few other innovations Baird succeeded in transmitting the shadow of a cross over a few feet. A start had been made.

The confidence gained from this initial simple image led immediately to follow up innovations. Baird had gathered together a small band of helpers who shared his enthusiasm. Together they helped to assemble the improvements that were needed for further progress. The cardboard disks were replaced by more solid structures as seen in the illustration below. It will be noticed that down the length of the image of the head are a series of slightly curved lines, each line produced by focussing the image on to the selenium cell through the successive spiral of holes during the rotation of the disc. In fact there were two half spirals enabling two frames per rotation. Shading of the image along each line was to be achieved later by a second disc having peripheral holes similar to the other disc but travelling very much faster so that the gradations of shade can change as the line progresses. Thus two frames are built up for each rotation of the slower disc. To prevent flicker thirty lines per frame at twelve and a half frames per second were found to be the minimum required; although the initial shadow image was five frames per second. These speeds were increased as the development progressed to achieve superior picture resolution.

A system of line interlacing was developed and later used to introduce colour television by interlacing filters of the three primary colours per frame producing colour TV three or four decades ahead of its ultimate introduction.

One problem remained to be overcome to realise clear moving images. There is a slight delay in the build-up of current in the selenium call - slight in this context meaning a few milliseconds. This was one of the many problems that others who were attempting to develop television were struggling with. Baird overcame this by the use of a transformer coupled amplifier for the current produced by the call. The rate of change of current in the inductance: i.e the coils of the transformer was used by Baird to compensate for the current lag in the cell – just another example of timely innovation.

A further, later interesting innovation was seeing in the dark. Instead of the image being illuminated by conventional light it was illuminated by infrared radiation. Whilst this was of interest as a novelty, it had no other interest at that time due to the lack of sensitivity of the infrared sensors. It is now used extensively for night surveillance.

In 1926 he also took out a patent in which televised objects were viewed by very short radio waves, a precursor of Radar later developed by Sir Robert Watson-Watt and others.

Just over a year after moving to Hastings, Baird demonstrated to the Radio Times magazine that it was possible to transmit moving silhouette images with his early apparatus. His activities were starting to be noticed, but not appreciated by everyone, in particular by his landlord in Hastings who gave him notice to quit. In late 1924 he returned to London, and set up a laboratory in an attic in Soho.

The break came when with help from a surprise source, following an advertisement for financial help for an inventor "to develop apparatus for seeing by wireless." He was visited by Mr Selfridge junior, who having heard of his ability to "see through a wall," suggested he might like to give a demonstration at the Selfridges store as part of its celebrations in January 1925. The demonstration showing the transmission of shadow images went on for three weeks leaving Baird exhausted and laid up for the following weeks.

Later in October 1925 he achieved true television pictures with graduations of light and shade, a great improvement on earlier results which were silhouettes. In January 1924 he held a widely publicise demonstration in his laboratory to members of the Royal Institution. This gave him the credibility he so badly needed, enabling him to raise the capital required to set up Baird television Ltd, financed primarily by Gaumont British, a major player in the cinema industry at that time.

With television now established in the laboratory Baird was now in a position to show its full potential. He astounded the world first by transmitting television from London to Glasgow in 1927 and following it in 1928 by transmitting across the Atlantic to a receiver in New York giving him further the credibility he so badly needed, enabling him to raise the capital required for his new company in 1927.

Having a complete monopoly of television the company started producing regular television programmes from its premises in Long Acre in 1929 for broadcast over the BBC's transmitters. The BBC insisted on regarding these programmes as experimental, but it could be said that television had arrived. Baird through dogged perseverance had achieved his goal; nevertheless he continued innovate extending his attention to the cinema, in 1931 making the first live transmission of the Derby to a screen at the London Coliseum.

Even more remarkable was the demonstration of colour television in 1928 by interlacing the three primary colours using three additional spinning discs at the transmitter and receiver. This preceded commercial transmissions by five decades. In 1944 he was able to demonstrate colour displayed on a cathode ray tube.

In fact it was in part due to the success of Baird's work that led to his failure to capitalise on his brilliant television developments; recognised by some of the greatest scientists of the day, namely by Sir Edward Appleton, whose notable work was the defining of the characteristics of the ionisation layer named after him, Professor Sir Oliver Lodge who, shortly after Marconi developed wireless telegraphy, established the means of frequency channel spacing by defining the resonant circuit, and even recognition by the prime minister of the day, Ramsay Macdonald.

It was the commercial establishment with their behind the scenes activities that frustrated Baird; aided and abetted by Lord Reith's unaccountable dislike of television; or perhaps the great man preferred dealing with the major players in the radio industries; such as Marconi-EMI in this country with their links to the internationally powerful Radio Corporation of America which dominated the radio industry word-wide, well aware that Television was the future of the industry. Baird's innovative skill did not extend to financial machinations or power politics. Nevertheless his company were broadcasting regular programs from their studio in Long acre during 1928/1929, and were having considerable success in Germany prior to the rise of Adolph Hitler.

Initially the approach to the BBC to broadcast television through their transmitters was turned down flat. However a parliamentary committee was set up to assess the broadcasting of television by the BBC. It made such a recommendation. It was not well received by the BBC, grudgingly allowing transmissions for half an hour after the close down of their regular sound transmissions at 11 pm. Furthermore

Baird Television had to pay for the use of the BBC transmitters, whereas in other countries, such as the USA, the television companies were paid for their programme transmissions.

Baird was very encouraged by a very different attitude in the USA during a short visit in 1931. He found that big business was able and willing to invest large sums of money with a view to later profits from commercials, and with this in mind there appeared to be many opportunities for Baird, and indeed many offers. However the "not invented here" attitude of the massive radio conglomerates used their lobbying power to prevent such offers coming to fruition.

The BBC later took over the Baird equipment to broadcast their own programmes, for which they paid nothing; later taking the credit for the broadcasting of television! It was another sixty years before colour television, first demonstrated by Baird in 1928, was to be broadcast. What a waste of such innovative talent and Intellectual Capital!

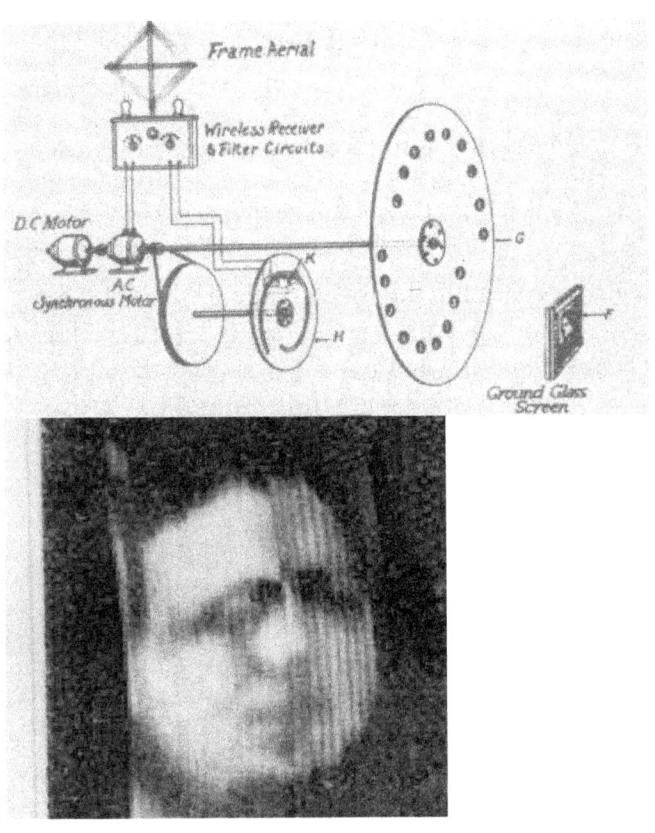

CHAPTER 3

Malcolm Baird looks back over 60 years

Science, Innovation and Attitudes

Mention has already been made of the false dawn of the swinging sixties. Prime Minister Harold MacMillan's statement that' you've never had it so good' ranks with Harold Wilson's pronouncement, a decade or so later, of the coming of the White Heat of Technology. Unfortunately the technology fled across the oceans, both West and East

Professor Malcolm Baird comments that the climate of that time was not very encouraging referring to these sad and moving lines that echo down the years, written by John Bolton on his time with a small pharmaceutical company taken over by a much larger Company. His lament of 1962 seems appropriate:

Death of a Laboratory:

The one, the heaven sent, the spark-of-the-morning invention
Does not invariably strike on the benches of the strong battalions,
Along the polished corridors where the meticulous salary scales
flow
Where the modulated pension scheme lives, breathing on the firm
foundation
Of a Lombard Street bank grounded in the firmest mountain rock.
It came to you, here, underpaid, despised, unknown
To you here, hidden in an industrial slum, here
Where the professors, the leaders of industry, grown
To magnificence on fat years of boom, had for all these years
Written off their trim maps of what had been and what was yet to
come.

Malcolm Baird continues:

"The popular image of science and technology was strong in the post war years, but behind the facade all was not well. My course in Applied Chemistry at Glasgow University took me to aging factories which brought to mind William Blake's phrase ...*among those dark satanic mills.* In the summer of 1955 I spent three months in a margarine factory. Even to my untutored eye the equipment seemed to be worn out and there were process inefficiencies. But when I mentioned these in my visit report I was firmly told by the general manager that this was the way they had always done things and they were not about to change because of what a student said. No attempt was made to answer my

37

specific points and I did not have the nerve to press them."

"Taken on the whole, the 1950s and 1960s were lost decades for Britain's industrial progress. This was due to a combination of greed, complacency and failure to meet foreign competition. It was common for BBC newsreaders to refer to "both sides of industry", as if it was a battlefield between unions and management. The 1960s were marked by closures of innumerable Scottish factories, mines and shipyards."

Anti-science culture

"Research and innovation were often seen as destroying jobs rather than saving them. The fear of science has its roots in the middle ages when it was seen as a form of sorcery."

"Matters improved in 1660 with the formation of the Royal Society under the auspices of Charles the Second. However, there was still a residual distrust, even as the industrial revolution began to accelerate human progress. Poets such as William Slake were repelled by heavy industry while Victorian society tacitly assumed that science and engineering were not fit occupations for a gentleman, far less for a lady. Engineers were perceived as uncouth characters."

"As late as the 1950s, the influential public schools and the older universities encouraged the study of classics and humanities as ingredients for the well-rounded character, but had little to say in favour of science. Winston Churchill's scientific aide, Professor Lindeman (a.k.a. Lord Cherwell), met with stiff opposition to his idea for an Oxbridge college which emphasised science and technology; but eventually the go-ahead was given for the formation of Churchill College Cambridge, with major support from the government and the Ford Motor Company. The inaugural tree-planting in 1959 in a field on the western outskirts of the city the 84-year-old Churchill was given a silver shovel with which he energetically threw earth over the tree roots and over the feet of the nearby dignitaries, who hastily took a step back."

"Since 1945 most of the industrialised western states have followed a social democratic policy, providing security in various forms: a health service, pensions, unemployment insurance and, as a last resort, welfare. All this was coupled until recently with very high rates of progressive income tax. This led to an anti-capitalist and risk-adverse culture in which one was not encouraged to stick one's neck out. Interviewers from big companies were for well-rounded team players and they extolled their pension plans, assuming that a career with their company was a career for life."

Risk and politics
"Since 1945 most of the industrialised western states have followed a social democratic policy, providing security in various forms: a health service, pensions, unemployment insurance and, as a last resort, welfare. All this was coupled until recently with very high rates of

39

progressive income tax. This led to an anti-capitalist and risk-averse culture in which one was not encouraged to stick one's neck out. Interviewers from big companies like Shell and ICI told me that they were looking for well-rounded team players and they extolled their pension plans, assuming that a career with their company was a career for life."

"The demands of innovation are not the same as those of a long-term job with a large company. The "team player" must also have the competitive qualities of the "solo player" and a willingness to take risks. Although the wealthy investor is accustomed to risk and can afford to "win a few or lose a few", ordinary people who are trying to start a small business do not have enough capital to cover any mistakes. Such enterprising individuals deserve encouragement which is not always forthcoming. Big lenders such as the banks prefer to invest their money in safer assets such as property, which has steadily appreciated for as long as most of us can remember. Industrial properties (factories) were the exception, although the land that they occupied has kept its value."

"The British film industry which had promoted science and technology sixty years ago is a shadow of what it was. Television coverage of science has moved into the realm of fantasy with such shows as Dr Who, while scientific documentaries are dominated by overexcited {and overpaid) presenters who project their personalities at the expense of the information they try to convey."

The universities – pure verses applied:

"Innovations usually have a scientific or technical basis; however it is sadly true that in the last 50 years large companies have closed or cut back their corporate research laboratories. The largest remaining concentrations of scientific and engineering talent are the universities, where innovation is being encouraged by new patterns of research funding."

"Modern science, as we know it dates back to the formation of the Royal Society in 1660. This led to a transformation of research from a sort of "secret wizardry" towards a free exchange and discussion of results and ideas. The main vehicle for this was the scientific journal. Some of today's scientific journals go back to the 17th century, while new journals are continuously being created as science expanding to new subject areas."

"A scientist normally writes his/her research results and sends them to a journal for publication. Before the paper is accepted it is independently and expertly reviewed (peer reviewed) to ensure originality and clarity. Reviewers expect that the paper should give enough detail about the experiment to make it possible for someone else to repeat it and check its findings. This system has been enormously successful over the past 350 years. Scientific progress has been made by a kind of multiple international game of tennis, with players (scientists) lobbing their ideas and stimulated creativity leading to steady progress with the ultimate peak of international scientific achievement being the Nobel Prize. Alfred

Nobel himself was a supremely successful innovator but he recognised the value of pure science. On the other hand there is no Nobel prize for engineering!"

Secrecy

"The widespread introduction of secrecy in university research could damage the process of international scientific exchange that has been so successful for 300 years. It may also result in a return the old perception of scientists as sorcerers and wizards. The cynic could argue that this is already happening with *Dr Who*. However the truth is that science and engineering are demanding professions which depend heavily on a combination of common sense, intelligence and honesty. More than 98% of the scientists and engineers that I have met have had these qualities."

The "purity" of science

"Some university scientists have a disdain for commercial applications as opposed to the pure disinterested search for knowledge *per se*. Although this rather snobbish knowledge is becoming outdated it is still to be found here and there. At the height of the industrial revolution the Oxford mathematician Professor J S Smith (1825-1883) remarked in one of his lectures.

it is a peculiar beauty of this method, gentlemen, and one which really endears it to the scientific mind, that under no circumstances can it be of the smallest possible utility.

"A century later the scientist and novelist C P Snow wrote:"

Scientific industry is the refuge of the not-quite-good-enough (which is why industrial thousands are wasted on research).

"On the industrial side Dr Clifford C Paterson (1879-1948), the research director of the General Electric Company, wrote bitterly in his wartime diary about the difficulty of working with academic physicists in the radar programme of World War 11:"

I have the impression from various sources that our academic radar effort is poisoned with intrigue, jealousy and un-charitableness. Industrial and commercial life seems clean in comparison. (May16 1941)."

Agreed, some, but not all, were very prickly!" - author.

Individual verses corporate innovation

There is a belief that following the latest spectacular discoveries, in particular in the realm of Information Technology, rob all pertinence of previous perceptions of innovation by individuals. This surely is too narrow a view as witnessed in chapter 4. which witnesses a remarkable example of individual innovation, far removed from "High Tech" – shipping.

Professor Baird refers to an article by Professor John Jewkes as early as 1958 querying this assumption that we are now dominated by the belief that technical progress can only come from mass attacks upon set problems. Traditionally much pioneering inventions were carried out from the innovative work of those working on their own behalf with limited resources and often limited scientific knowledge. Again Einstein's quote comes to mind, "Imagination is more important than Knowledge."

"Professor Jewkes notes:
"We are now dominated by the doctrine that technical progress can come only from mass attacks upon set problems. Yet much technical progress has come through independent enthusiasts working with limited resources under discouraging conditions and for long ridiculed or ignored by the main bodies of organized science

and technology; by men who were working on their own behalf without the backing of research institutions and often with limited resources and assistance or, where the inventors were employed in institutions, these institutions were, as in the case of universities, of such a kind that the individuals were autonomous."

"The autonomy of universities can be threatened by too much dependence on grants for specific purposes"

"Men with great powers of originality are in many ways a race apart. Like any other group, of course, they differ between themselves, but on the whole they are constitutionally more averse to cooperation than the rest of us. 'I am a horse for single harness,' wrote Einstein, 'and not cut out for landau or teamwork.' This follows because their great gifts arise from the habit of calling everything, even the simplest assumptions, into question; because they are in the grip of inner compulsions which lead them to assume the right of deciding how their special powers should be employed and how best a task should be approached, to resent interference, and to be thrown out of balance by it. Many of them are, by temperament, wholly unsuitable for work in any research institution which is formally organized. And, beyond that, it is even conceivable that, in many cases, their native powers of innovation might be weakened or destroyed by over-prolonged scientific or technical education."

"Although Vladimir Zworkin was an employee of the Radio Corporation of America many other important innovation leading to the invention of television were made by another American, Farnsworth, working independently, and the first complete system for television broadcasting was created for the British Broadcasting Corporation by a British firm, Baird Television, of modest size."

Note by the author:

This takes us on to Team work. Is the importance of "A good Team Player" exaggerated? Ok, in a modern supermarket perhaps, but it carries with it a countervailing loss when looking for mutual understanding and the loss is greater the larger the team. A large team is basically a committee, and as pointed out in "Parkinson's Law," has no time for hunches and intuitions, only a common consensus.

The author recalls viewing an example of this whilst visiting the Smithsonian museum in Washington. There was a record of the work of a committee set up during the first decade of the twentieth century to carry out investigations into heavier than air flying machines. Extensive trails failed to give a result. The Wright brothers working alone achieved it. It is doubted if they had committee meetings or lengthy progress reports.

In the Bell Labs, a large and well known research establishment, the development of the first transistor was carried out by a group of three each of whom were dedicated to the same goal. This togetherness turned to competitiveness following the world wide publicity that followed, in turn producing a dramatic improvement of the original point contact transistor by the leader of the group, William Shockley working in secret; thereafter jealousy broke up the group!

The author, while part of a large multinational corporation (ITT) ran three separate development groups.

1. Microwave antennas, aircraft receivers, and transmitter sources with two specialist development engineers
2. Height and distance measurement project with three development engineers
3. Specialised circuits: Four circuit development engineers, including author.

Two Research and Development Engineers outside the author's "Top Field" Laboratory with a prototype of the FM/CW Radio Altimeter to be used in conjunction with the first Automatic landing to be made with fare paying passengers in zero visibility.

Many innovative circuits had to be developed to overcome problems such as "double bounce" with its associated nose down demand on the approach to touchdown, and signal fading at maximum height. John Lee, on the left of the picture, holds a joint patent with the author for an "electronic flywheel" and went on to join STL Laboratories.

All worked well with small dedicated teams until there was a possibility of world-wide business when the parent company sent outside specialists, including a vice-president who tried to control development with a pert chart! OK perhaps if we were building a bridge. The smooth running of the group descended into a nightmare. One foreign contract was obtained before the parent company closed down its UK operation.

CHAPTER 4

Background to the Port of Felixstowe

Colonel Tomline, 1813-1889

The small and relatively unknown dock basin at Felixstowe was the brain child Colonel Tomline in the mid-eighteen-eighties; a wealthy local landowner, who had no time for merely giving money to charitable handouts; which might well give self-esteem to the donor, did little for the self-esteem of the recipient. "It was," the colonel said, "the duty of the rich to provide work to the poor." And so it was that the Felixstowe Dock and Railway Company came into existence.

Yet the construction of the original dock in the 1880s was no mean feat. Ridiculed by bankers and business colleagues as a waste of money the Colonel decided to fund it himself, much to the scepticism of his colleagues in high places, one of which was none other than the home secretary of that time, Sir Robert Peel.

Educated at Eton alongside Gladstone he was one of the ten largest landowners in the country. He was also an active member of parliament and together with Gladstone supported Robert Peel's reform of the Corn Laws.

In 1867 the colonel purchased six thousand acres of farm land in the Walton-Felixstowe area of Suffolk; included in this was about a thousand acres of shore and saltings, useless for agriculture. This land he believed could be opened up as a seaside resort and a dock could be built on the opposite side of Harwich Harbour to rival the Port of Harwich, providing work for those who might otherwise be without income. It was also noted by some that the good people of Harwich had recently rejected the attempt by the colonel to become their MP!

First access would need to be improved. The main road from Ipswich ended at the village of Walton a few miles short of Felixstowe which was at that time mainly given over to farming. Furthermore the Walton-Felixstowe area formed an 'inland peninsular'; bounded on the South by Harwich Harbour and the River Orwell as far as Ipswich, and on the North by the River Deben as far as Woodbridge.

Colonel Tomline would build his own railway to connect with Ipswich. On being told that the investment in the railway was not likely to make any money Tomline was said to reply that it was better than spending it at the Newmarket races.

Wealthy or not Colonel Tomline did not have an easy ride. The first proposal to build the railway line along the shore of the River Orwell met with stiff opposition including the owner of Broke Hall in the village of Nacton claiming it would cut the flight line of ducks to his duck decoy. However in 1875 the Felixstowe Railway and Pier Act enabled the Felixstowe Railway and Pier Company to make and maintain a pier plus a connecting railway via an alternative route.

Colonel Tomline was elected chairman of the new company. It was soon clear that he who pays the piper calls the tune; all decisions, right or mistaken, were taken by the colonel. The railway cost £106,000. Three locomotives were ordered together with coaches and goods trucks. The line joined the Great Eastern line to Ipswich and London at Westerfield Junction, just outside Ipswich. The first train that left Westerfield in 1877 was pulled by a bright new locomotive named Tomline.

An early passenger train belonging to the
Felixstowe Railway and Dock Company

Travellers on the train might have noticed
that at every level crossing there was a house
built on each side if the track; one was for the
gatekeeper and the other for a platelayer – not
strictly necessary but no doubt part of the good
colonel's philanthropy.

At a meeting of the directors in November
of 1875 application to parliament for a bill
authorising the company to construct a tidal dock
basin and other works was agreed. Work began
in November 1881. It must have pleased Colonel
Tomline that the work was labour intensive.
Health and safety did not seem to be a problem.

The dock labour force posing for a picture

A Thames Barge unloading at a pier of
Felixstowe Dock. The outline of Harwich across
Harwich Harbour can be seen at the top of the
picture.

The dock was completed in 1886, the first trading vessel entering in November of that year.

A paddle steamer entering Felixstowe Dock in the 1920's; there was a regular service between Felixstowe, Harwich and Ipswich.

From the very beginning Colonel Tomline's efforts were thwarted by the powerful Great Eastern Railway Company that controlled the rail route to London and successfully blocked efforts by the dock company to extend the rail link to the Midlands, the Great Eastern having links with not only the Port of Harwich, but Hull and other East coast ports. When the company applied for a Parliamentary Bill for using, maintaining or working Steam Vessels between Felixstowe and ports on the continent opposition came from, amongst others, the Member of Parliament for Hull, who, following the defeat of the bill, remarked that the Great Eastern Railway was using its powers in a manner that was against the interest of the country; crushing private enterprise by their monopoly. This attitude was to continue throughout the rest of the century and beyond.

Colonel Tomline died in 1889, never to see his dream realised. The visit of Augusta Victoria, Empress of Germany Queen of Prussia, for a holiday in 1891 did more for the reputation of Felixstowe as a seaside resort than the colonels well-meaning activities. However it must be said that without the building of the dock and associated rail link the Port of Felixstowe may not have materialised.

CHAPTER 5

Innovation through Intelligence Capital

Felixstowe dock pre-World-war 11. The outline
of Harwich can be seen across the harbour.

The euphoria of VE Day May 8th 1945
soon wore off. By contrast with the defeated
West Germany which pulling itself together and
rebuilding itself by concerted personal and
national determination, with generous assistance
from the United States through marshal aid, and
France which had built up its Industrial structure
by cooperating with Germany following German
occupation in 1940, the UK was in a state of
economic ruin continuing to experience relative
economic decline for decades to follow. Far
from benefitting from marshal aid, it was in debt
to the United States for the lease-lend
arrangements of the war.

West Germany had by the end of the
1950s doubled production from its pre-war levels

and the Italian economy was growing rapidly. France, modernising its industry, was becoming the dominant force in Europe.

The UK was bedevilled by political dogma, discouraging enterprise, the modernisation of industry struggling with old and worn out machine tools, preventing individual entrepreneurial activities and innovation until the arrival of the Morris Mini and the swinging sixties.

During this period there was one remarkable example of innovation carried forward by two remarkable entrepreneurs and innovators with determination against all the odds, transforming a small, derelict dock basin employing perhaps no mere than a couple of dozen to the first and largest container port in the UK employing 2,500 directly and up to 50,000 people indirectly. Furthermore this activity was carried out in the small town of Felixstowe.

Following the second world War, during which the dock had been the home of naval motor torpedo boats, the dock was in a parlous state, silted up, and very little used, except by few remaining sailing barges carrying grain to the adjacent mills, and a small passenger ferry connecting to Harwich and Shotley on the other side of Harwich Harbour.

The author's father had his boat moored at the far end of the dock – an old ships lifeboat, fitted out with an ancient Austin Seven motor, started by wrapping a strap round the flywheel and giving it a mighty pull! This was used for doing a bit of fishing and generally messing about in Harwich Harbour.

The saviour of the derelict dock basin came from an East Anglian agricultural merchant, Gordon Parker, engaged in the export of barley. Frustrated with the difficulties of exporting from existing ports, for instance at Kings Lynn, operating under the National Dock Labour Scheme, taking seventeen men with a crane to load 200 tons in a day; whereas at the small Norfolk port at Wells, where Gordon Parker had his own quayside silo and workers, he was able to load 300 tons in a day with just three men, Mr. Parker decided to find a better outlet to the continent.

Gordon Parker

Not only did Mr. Parker find an alternative port, he purchased it, together with the surrounding "useless" marsh-land for £50,000, becoming Chairman of the Felixstowe Dock and Railway Company. It was considered to be a hopeless investment, banks or government agencies refusing, to have anything to do with it. The refurbishment would be carried out by the small dock's own labour force; paid for by attracting such business as could be found.

Ironically some of the earliest income came from the ill-fated ground nuts scheme sponsored at great expense by the government of the day, enabling a trickle of the millions invested in this scheme by the taxpayer to help the cash strapped development of what was to become The Port of Felixstowe, for those nuts that were produced were stored in the refurbished sheds at Felixstowe dock. Further income, whilst the dock was being dredged, came from the storage of vegetable oil in the cleaned out World-War 1 admiralty oil tanks.

Just as the dock was beginning to look like a viable operation disaster struck. The storm of January 1953 broke through the sea defences sending millions of tons of sea water crashing through the dock, flooding the storage sheds, ruining the contents and damaging much of the dock structure.

Mr. Parker and his small workforce, undaunted, set about Mission Impossible, a recovery operation. He enlisted as his second in command Ian Trelawny, a man who had proved his leadership qualities as a senior officer at the Motor Torpedo Boat Flotilla based at the dock during the war.

Trelawny quotes: "looking back the impression that remains is the utter depression of the place. The dock basin was so silted up that the depth at low water was only six feet in places. The entrance was marked by two jagged rows of wooden piles, leaning drunkenly as the storm had left them."

"Fortunately I was too ignorant to share the misgivings of the many people who insisted that the enterprise was doomed to failure, and said it at every opportunity."

In spite of this depressing outlook, the dock company's tiny staff, numbering no more than thirty-two workers and office staff set to work with a will. Surely the story that follows is an epic, a masterpiece of improvisation and innovation.

"The early days were fantastic," says Trelawny. "We really didn't have any money; we had the greatest difficulty paying the wages every week. We lived literally hand to mouth. There was many a Friday morning on which we searched eagerly but often in vain, through the meagre post for a cheque that would enable us to pay the wages by 5 p.m. I remember one particular time when our wages bill was about £600 a week and on this particular morning it was a matter of going round dunning the few shipping we had in the port to no avail. On this occasion I borrowed the money. On other occasions Gordon Parker would provide the money from his own pocket"

"This lack of money was not allowed to stop the work. When the company's credit ran out with one supplier of the cement another source was found."

Dredging the dock was a priority, and many obstacles needed to be overcome, one of which Trelawny wryly recalls, "fruitless and frustrating correspondence passed to and fro between the dock company and government departments concerning a jetty installed while under wartime control and stood in the way of the dredger. One department after another denied any responsibility for the jetty. We couldn't afford the dredger to remain idle. So having telegraphed ultimata to everyone we could think of we harnessed our old tractor to the sea end of the jetty and with the dredger clearing the mud and giving the jetty an occasional nudge we dragged the whole lot ashore on to the waste ground behind the dock littered with discarded boom defence material, none of which was wasted but available for future use in the reclaiming land and building storage sheds around the Dock."

The dredging of the dock basin was completed in the winter of 1955. Concrete piles for the new piers were cast in the dock itself and were floated out on oil drums to where they were driven in by a pile driver mounted on two barges fastened together by steel girders. One of the barges was subsequently used to mount an old steam crane used for picking lumps of concrete and other rubbish out of the dock when the dock's own workforce constructed a new deep water quay at the east of the dock

The concrete and other spoil that was lifted out to increase the low water depth was not wasted, but washed and graded in the Company's own ballast plant or dumped in the waste ground to raise the level, providing reclaimed land that would prove useful as the facilities were expanded.

Ballast was a commodity that the impecunious dock company could ill afford to buy. One way of overcoming this expense was to obtain a contract to break up runways and perimeter tracks on some of the wartime airfields in East Anglia. The concrete and much other material from this demolition work was used as hard-core for roads and building foundations in the Dock area. Demolished buildings could be re-erected as dock warehouses and transport sheds.

Labour troubles at the traditional docks worked to the advantage of The Felixstowe Dock Company. Shipping companies were beginning to appreciate the efficiency of the handling of cargo together with the labour stability at Felixstowe. The first of these was the General

Steam Navigational Company, setting up their own office at the dock; .others followed.

Good business was to be obtained from tank storage. To do this it was necessary to clean out the vegetable oils that had been stored in the former Admiralty tanks. Steam from one of the old steam cranes was used to heat the residue of the oil, thinning it sufficiently to be run out of the tank; however it could not clear the congealed oil from the sides. Workers had to get into the tanks through an inspection hole, and erect scaffolding inside the tank to remove the thick sticky oil adhering to the sides.

Ian Trelawny, responding to the upsurge of the plastics industry, secured business to send solvents through Felixstowe. This necessitated the construction of a second tank farm. There was considerable local opposition to this; in particular from the author's father-in-law, a retired surveyor and civil engineer who had retired to Felixstowe and been elected to the local council. He went on local radio to voice his concern at the danger of storing petroleum products close to the new housing estates being built on the reclaimed marsh land expanding towards the river and dock area. However these fears were overcome and the last tank was still not completed when the first ship arrived to unload. Trelawny tells the story:

"To cash in on considerable interest aroused in the chemical trade by this innovation we decided to hold a reception in the Little Ships

Hotel to celebrate the first shipload. The great day dawned, but the work on the new and very special tanks was not quite complete. The tanker was reported off the Sunk light vessel (off the Felixstowe coast), then entering the harbour, and then approaching the dock entrance. Welding on the tanks went on in a desperate race against time."

"Our guests were retained by evermore bounteous hospitality from leaving the hotel until the tanker berthed."

"Once again fortune smiled on us in the nick of time; the tanker ran aground, only mildly aground, but just sufficient to give us time to complete the last weld just before the re-floated ship birthed."

"Now our guest were at last permitted, even invited and in some cases persuaded to emerge into the daylight and were impressed by the efficiency of the berthing and pipeline coupling operation, the gleaming new tanks and most of all by the extent of the hospitality!"

"The wisdom of having sought to cater for the solvents trade was shown when it increased by a factor of four in six years. Such was the growth of this business that in 1961 a subsidiary company, Felixstowe Tank Developments Ltd. was formed. Since then an area of approximately ten hectares has been developed for the storage and handling of all kinds of bulk liquids; some of the major oil companies installing their own facilities."

"Tank Freight Ltd, which operates a fleet of more than 600 road tankers, purchased a controlling interest in Felixstowe Tank Developments, the dock company keeping a 20% interest. The new capital enabled development to continue." "Initiatives and innovations were adopted to attract the general cargo trade, which in the fifties was still being carried on in much the same way as for generations past."

Felixstowe pioneered new handling techniques which were to revolutionise the shipping, and ports industry.

While Dockers in the major ports resisted new methods and continued with old and outmoded practices, the expanding workforce at Felixstowe Dock, almost entirely recruited from the surrounding area welcomed the new methods that speeded up cargo handling enabling quicker turn around which was appreciated by both shippers and ship-owners. One such company was the Danish brewery, Carlsberg, shipping fifty million bottles a year with negligible losses.

"We were innovator's par excellence," says Ian Trelawny. "Much of the new equipment was built by members of the dock company team. "If we couldn't afford to buy an item, we made it, if a piece of equipment we needed didn't exist, we invented it."

"Much of the sophisticated cargo handling equipment so nonchalantly accepted in ports throughout the world today was conceived in the canteen, or long after working hours.

Many a night was spent in devising, trying, reconstructing and trying again until it was got right."

"We had tremendous support from all the personnel. I didn't think up things alone. When it came to operating the roll-on, roll off service the drivers redesigned the tractor units to suit".

"With the growing business went growing expansion."

"The next milestone was the development of facilities for the handling of container traffic"

"The change of loading 20 ft. Containers which had been packed at the factory and would not be unpacked until they arrived at their final destination meant creating new methods of moving these large boxes from ship to the articulated lorries; Felixstowe led the way. A container could be picked up in 20 seconds and moved clear in 24 seconds."

As early as 1967 the port was handling 18,522 containers; by the following year 74,033. Between 1963 and 1969 the number of ships handled at the port rose from 1,183 to 3,109, the tonnage from 341,812 to 2,715,664.

Initially the port was built up on cargo trade. In 1965 negotiations with The Transport Ferry Service, an operation started by Lieutenant Colonel Bustard in 1946 using redundant tank landing craft resulted in the provision of a roll-on, roll-off births for the use of larger ferries coming into service.

Continued expansion in the 70s was now proving a problem. From an almost unnoticed small dock the Port of Felixstowe and its success was getting noticed.

There was talk that the port should be nationalised and brought into line with other large British ports. Rampant inflation was making it difficult to raise the capital needed for further expansion. Profits alone no longer seemed sufficient to provide for the further expansion needed for the 21st century. In 1976, to counter this situation, Gordon Parker persuaded the shareholders to accept a bid of around five million pounds from European Ferries for the Felixstowe Dock Company together with an investment of around £700,000 for continued development; thus securing the future of the port. With further investments of several million pounds the small Felixtowe dock basin evolved into the largest Port in the British Isles and one of the largest in the world – a pretty good return for an initial investment of £50,000.

In 1991 the majority holding was purchased by Hutchinson Whampoa for £90,000,000, and in 1994 had an estimated share value of £130,000,000.

Following the purchase of the company by European Ferries in 1976 Mr. Gordon Parker was made life president. Ian Trelawny continued his work as head of the company's consultation service advising on container ports all over the world.

Ian Trelawny laying the foundation stone of
the office block that bears his name to this day

As a footnote, whilst the author was
visiting his sister in a sheltered housing flat in
Felixstowe on the occasion of her 95th birthday
he met a neighbour, Andy Anderson, who had
worked at the port for over twenty years,
completing his service managing traffic at the
roll-on roll-off terminal. On completion of the
enlargement of the berths in 1979, part of the
investment by the new owners, Princess Anne
came to open the new passenger terminal. Andy

was one of ten operatives of the terminal chosen to welcome her on the roll-on bridge. Andy was ninth in line. The Princess asked each one where they were from. Everyone appeared to come came from elsewhere other than Felixstowe until she came to Andy's neighbour, R Summars, who was black. She obviously expected an answer such as The Bahamas. "Felixstowe", he responded." He was born and bred within sight of the dock!

CHAPTER 6

People Capital

The building of the Dock

The marshes behind the dock basin before they were reclaimed and concreted as the sight for part of the Tank Farm. The author and his cousin John used to catch tadpole and newts in the ditches to take home in jars, puting them in water buts, to watch them grow.

Part of the Tank Farm behind the original dock basin, seen on the top right hand of the picture, built on the marshland reclaimed using dredged spoil from the dock, broken conconcrete from unused wartime runways together with any other remains of unwanted dilapidated buildings and structures. The tank farm was expanded to cater for the increasing trade in chemical solvents, in particular those related to the growing plastics industry. The original, though expanded dock basin can be seen in the top right hand corner

Building extra tanks to accomodate chemical solvents

A busy time loading lorries in the early 60's. Signs of thing to come can be seen with just two containers at the centre right of the picture

Unbelievably fork lift trucks were banned in the major port in the National Dock Labour Scheme.. A counter productive measure leading to major shipping companies diverting traffic to the new and more efficiant Port of Felixstowe.

The first container terminal, completed in the mid 60's, can be seen in the foreground. Note the tanker discharging at the jetty just North of the original dock basin.

Two additional container jetties able to lift a container from ship to lorry in 45 seconds.

The installation of running gear for use with container freight trains, relieving the road traffic by around a third.

Still undergoing further expansion!

CHAPTER 7

Background to the end of an era

Boole, Babbage and De Morgan

GeorgeBoole
(1791-1871)

Charles Babbage
(17911-871)

In engineering or scientific terminology the conclusion of the 'swinging sixties' could be regarded as the 'beginning of the beginning' of the end of the mainly analogue era and the beginning of a new era; social and moral changes taking place during the sixties coinciding with the advent of the digital computer into the public domain affecting the way we live.

Was this epoch changing development the result of a flash of inspiration or insight of some brilliant innovator? Although many applications may have been the result of great entrepreneurial activity the brainchild of digital logic used in the modern computer goes back to the mathematician, philosopher and logician, George Boole, more than a hundred years earlier. Indeed it could be said to go back to Aristotle, for it was Aristotelian logic that Boole was involved in formalising at the time.

He considered mathematics as a tool for logic; using binary mathematics to express every logical statement as TRUE or FALSE, as "Turing Engines" do today.

Although Boole could not foresee the practical "hardware" that would result from his work a hundred years later he did appreciate the importance of it, writing in 1851:

"I am now about to set seriously to work upon preparing for the press an account of my theory of Logic and probabilities which in its present state I look upon as the most valuable if not the only valuable contribution that I have made or am likely to make to Science and the thing by which I would desire if at all to be remembered..."

His desire was granted. Boolean algebra based on his logic, is, and always will be, taught as the building block for computer programming in machine language and for data transmission on the internet.

The work he was publishing was An Investigation into the Laws of Thought, on which are founded the Mathematical Theories of Logic and Probabilities. This may sound rather remote from the operation of a computer, but the logic fitted perfectly with Alan Turing's definition of a Turing Machine that could be programmed to simulate logical activities in the same way as a human; for instance it could be programmed to play a game of chess (or in to-days popular games poker) in the same way as a human, and indeed has subsequently done just that. Specialised Turing machines can now assemble and paint cars on a mass production line, the instructions being in the form of Boolean algebra.

Boole's status as a mathematician, who together with Clerk-Maxwell is considered by some close to that of Einstein, is remarkable considering he had only a rudimentary elementary education. However his father, a shoemaker in Lincoln, had a fascination with mathematics which he passed on to his son who was mainly self-taught, not only in mathematics, but after being given tuition in Latin went on to teach himself Greek and modern languages.

At the tender age of 16 the young Boole was precluded from any further formal education due to the collapse of his father's business, and became the family breadwinner, taking up an appointment as a junior teacher in Doncaster. By the time he was nineteen he had opened his own school in Waddington near Lincoln, and at the age of 23 took over the running of Hall's Academy in Lincoln, which took in both day and boarding pupils, enabling employment for the rest of the family.

Despite what must have been an onerous task Boole maintained his interest and absorption in mathematics, studying the work of contemporary mathematicians, contributing himself to the Cambridge Mathematical Journal and communicating with other mathematicians of the day one of which was Augustus De Morgan, who is quoted as saying:

Boole's system of logic is but one of many proofs of genius and patience combined. ... That the symbolic processes of algebra, invented as tools of numerical calculation, should be competent to express every act of thought, and to furnish the grammar and dictionary of an all-containing system of logic, would not have been believed until it was proved.

De Morgan was also one of Boole's sponsors for his appointment to the chair of mathematics at Queens College, Cork in in 1849 writing:

I can speak confidently to the fact of his being not only well-versed in the highest branches of mathematics, but possessed of original power for their extension which gives him a very respectable rank among their English cultivators of this day.

George Boole remained at Cork for thirty years. Whilst there he married Mary Everest, the niece of Sir George Everest, after whom Mount Everest was named. Mary Boole, a mathematician in her own right, outlived her husband by some fifty years. They had five daughters, each of whom was associated with academic careers.

De Morgan's equations further extended Boolean algebra. The closeness of Boole's association with De Morgan over his thirty years at Cork is illustrated in 1850, Boole, writing to De Morgan:

If you should hear of any situation in England that would be likely to suit me let me know of it. I am terrified by the religious bigotry which is at the present raging round us here. I am not dissatisfied with my duties and may venture to say that I am on good terms with my colleagues and with my pupils. But I cannot help entertaining a feeling that recent events in the college have had the foundation of a lack of mutual trust and confidence among us.

The "troubles" in Ireland are nothing new!

Other mathematicians contemporary with Boole apart from Augustus de Morgan were Charles Babbage and, at a slightly later date, James Clerk Maxwell, the subject of a later chapter. The work of all four of these eminent mathematicians, logicians and physicists defined the essential ingredients of the internet.

The tragedy of Boole's early death has been described as follows:-

One day in 1864 *he walked from his residence to the College, a distance of two miles, in the drenching rain, and lectured in wet clothes. The result was a feverish cold which soon fell upon his lungs and terminated his career.*

It transpired that Boole's wife believed that a remedy should resemble the cause. She put Boole to bed and threw buckets of water over the bed since his illness had been caused by getting wet.

George Boole took no part in the construction of the Babbage Difference Machine although there was a connection through Mary Boole whose uncle, Sir .George Everest, is believed to have introduced Babbage to Indian logic in 1820.

Babbage certainly had a wide range of interests. After studying the haphazard postal service he recommended a uniform service resulting in the creation of the penny post, which continued more or less unchanged for 99 years; indeed the author can remember it being increased to 1½ pence in 1939.

He was involved in code-breaking during the Crimean war in 1850. He had interests in metrology and the improvement of data for the Nautical Almanac with a project to produce an encyclopaedic almanac of numeric information; his paper On Tables of the Constants of Nature and Art was printed by the Smithsonian Institution in 1856.

As a member of the British Association he clashed with members, identifying with industrialists rather than the rather stuffy attitudes of the academics who believed research should be confined to the universities and had no place in society, leading to his resignation.

He upset the Clergy with his publication of The North Bridgewater Treatises titled On the Power, Wisdom and Goodness of God advocating that God had the omnipotence to make laws to produce new species as required rather than interfere with miracles!

He hated the noise of organ grinders, Top of the Pops equivalent of the time, and had a distaste for commoners; being denounced in the

House of Commons for campaigning against the trundling of hoops, as by children in the streets! He applied twice for election to the House of Commons, but failed to get elected.

His Difference Machine first conceived as a programmed mechanical mathematical computer for producing tabular data for almanacs etc. was later extended as an analytical engine able to perform programmes presented to it on punched tape.

As mechanical engineer as well as a mathematician and philosopher (he advised Brunel on the building of the Great Western Railway), Babbage believed Analytical Engines would be able to help industrial design and manufacture. This was remarkable foresight a hundred years prior to computer programmes for Computer Aided Manufacture (CAM) and Computer Aided Design (CAD) – carried out with Boolean logic!

His interest in engineering extended to the analysis of manufacturing techniques in general, but in particular the inefficient use of skilled labour, advocating the division of labour, the precursor of modern day mass production

Babbage's outlook differed from that of Boole in that his academic achievements, although considerable, were directed towards engineering, machinery and manufacturing practices. He pointed out that skilled workers spent time working on tasks that could be carried out by less skilled labour, thus increasing production efficiency. He exposed the operation of cartels, particularly in the publishing trade, only recently to be broken. He was in agreement with Karl Marx who pointed out, correctly, that improvement in industrial efficiency was not for productivity, but for profit. Babbage's ideas on division of labour led to the unpopular introduction of the study of "time and motion" leading to mass production, pioneered, in particular, by Henry Ford.

The Babbage Difference Machine was never completed, although a replica has recently been built and shown to work as predicted.

Augustus De Morgan 1806-1879

The mid 1800s seem to have been a good time for logicians, for working in conjunction with Charles Boole was Augustus De Morgan. As many others who were to later achieve success and excellence in their vocation Augustus De Morgan, born in in Madras, India, the son of a colonel working in the East India Company in 1806, it was achieved in spite of disablement. He was born blind in one eye.

Like others at that time his schooling was deficient in mathematics, but with encouragement from a family friend he took an interest in Euclidean geometry. He entered Trinity College Cambridge at the age of sixteen, leaving as sixth wrangler.

He formalised Boolean Logic by defining its algebraic terms including "De Morgan's Theorems," which enabled the simplification of algorithms later used in the construction of complex computer programmes

The work of these three Mathematicians and logicians of the mid eighty's, remaining in the closets of the academic world for a hundred years, exploded into the public domain assuming a new importance at the dawn of the digital age. However they both covered a much wider field than that related to the background of the digital age. Boole, prior to his appointment as the first professor of mathematics at Queens College took an interest in local affairs supporting the early closing of shops, no longer applicable, and, with others, set up a building society to assist house ownership. He wrote treatises on differential calculus and Integration. He was also described as an excellent teacher and lecturer and, despite his severe countenance, a pleasant and genial character.

Augustus De Morgan, like Boole was a respected teacher. Unlike many university academics he believed in the dissertation of knowledge beyond the confines of academia. A member of the Society for the Diffusion of

Useful Knowledge he was one of its most, if not the most prolific and effective writers, much of it published in the Penny Cyclopaedia.

Finding the religious rigour of Oxford and Cambridge not to his liking De Morgan was active with others of founding the more liberal London University (.later named University College London), to be appointed the first professor of mathematics at the age of 22. His discourse on mental education contained in his introductory lecture is considered of importance to this day.

A lover of music he played the flute and was a popular performer at social occasions.

Both Boole and De Morgan have areas on the moon named after them.

It is ironic that in practice computers owe more to the work of Boole and De Morgan than of Babbage; not just influencing engineering and working practice but revolutionising it.

Unlike Boole and De Morgan Babbage was not noted for his teaching; he did no teaching!

Whilst this book is not concerned with technology some understanding of the term "digital" is appropriate. Those familiar with the technology may wish to skip the next chapter.

CHAPTER 8

Analogue to "Digital"

This chapter is a simplistic explanation of what is meant by the term Digital, as opposed to Analogue. For more specific information reference should be made to an appropriate text book.

Analogue:

Analogue can be defined in general as an object or quantity such as the position of the hands of a clock that represents another quantity; in this example time.

Prior to the digital era the sound volume of radios was controlled by the progressive rotation of a knob on the front of the set – analogue control.

In early land line telephones the varying air pressure sound from voice or music converts to electrical variations of the same frequency by the microphone and converted back to sound by the ear piece or loudspeaker. In modern phones the sound would be converted to digital format for transmission and back to analogue sound format at the receiver. Virtually any data can be converted into digital format; however it is invariably converted back to analogue after digital processing. The brain cannot process binary digital data.

Digital:

Digital logic as used in computers and the modern day transmission of data requires only two digits 1 and naught (not necessarily zero, though it can be). Thus it is a binary system, best illustrated by comparing the binary numbering system with the conventional decimal system.

Instead of shifting to an extra digit every additional power of 10 i.e. 9 to 10, 99 to 100, 999 to 1000, binary numbers use only ones and naughts, shifting to an extra digit every "times two" (powers of 2) as indicated in the following table, where naught does represent zero.

Decimal	Binary
	2^3 2^2 2^1 2^0 0
0	0
1	1
2	1 0
3	1 1
4	1 0 0
5	1 0 1
6	1 1 0
7	1 1 1
8	1 0 0 0
9	1 0 0 1
10	1 0 1 0
11	1 0 1 1
⋮	
16	1 0 0 0 0
17	1 0 0 0 1

Thus binary digits increase, in decimal number notation, at 2,4,8,16 32,64...

Electronically ones can be, and usually are, represented by a voltage above a defined threshold, typically two, and naught below a defined threshold, but not necessarily zero, due to the limitations of the electronic switches.

All Data in a digital computer (or mobile-phone or "app") also use only the digits one or naught. A memory may contain several million such digits - bits in computer technology. A computer memory may be said to have a capacity of a given number of Megabits or even Gigabits (1,000,000,000 bits). These can be accessed in microseconds due to the high switching speed of semiconductor electronic switches.

A computer needs to process these digits

Here we come to the work of the Logicians of the mid 1800s, in particular Boole and De Morgan. Boolean logic defined everything as TRUE or FALSE in algebraic terms.

In Boolean logic "1" stands for TRUE and "0" for FALSE: and as for binary numbers, 1 is a voltage above a defined threshold, and 0 a voltage below a defined threshold. This logic is processed in a computer using a special flow chart, usually called an algorithm when used for computer programming. Algorithms are not new. Euclid used them to solve geometric theorems around two thousand years ago.

Consider a process performed by a human, relative to a similar process performed by a programmed computer. A Turing Machine (modern computer) is said to be: "capable of being programmed to control a task in the same way as a human;" and that does include mechanical tasks such as assembling and paint spraying a car, but consider a simpler task such as a human making a telephone call illustrated in the following flow chart, or in computer terminology: Algorithm.

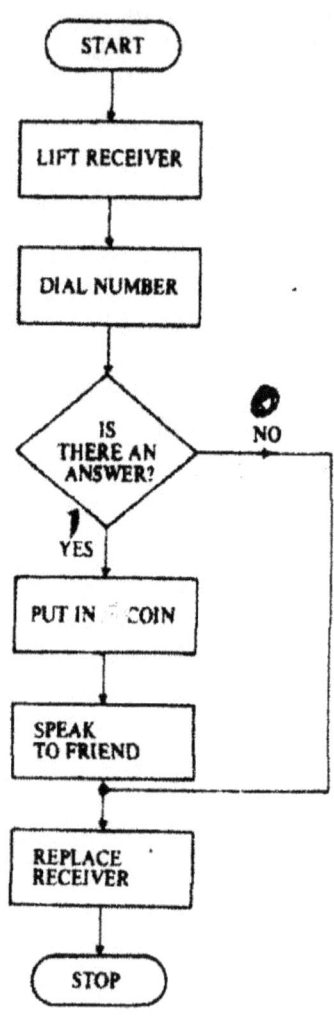

For a computer to perform this task it would probably substitute the task of "LIFT RECEVER" for "CONNECT TO SERVER", followed by "IS THERE A CNNECTION," if TRUE the caller would invariably have an account with the Server and would go directly to "SPEAK., However a computer is more likely to pass data, such as an Email, to another computer; in which case the task blocks could themselves consist of sub programs. A programme for a complex task could well consist of hundreds of sub programmes

A simpler example of an algorithm would be the opening of a remote automatic door only if both blue and red button are activated. Simplistically:

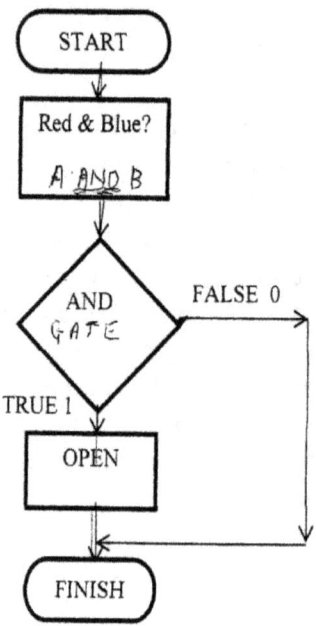

The switching of these logic terms is done by AND/OR "Logic Gates," best illustrated by the truth tables below. For example suppose input A of the AND gate in the diagram is the input from the blue button of the remote automatic door opener, and B from the red, the output will only be 1 when both A **AND** B are 1, as indicated in the "TRUTH TABLE" below." The diagrammatic illustrations of the switches indicate the action of the electronic switches within the gate.

<u>AND</u> Truth table:

A	B	output F
0	0	0
1	0	0
0	1	0
1	1	1

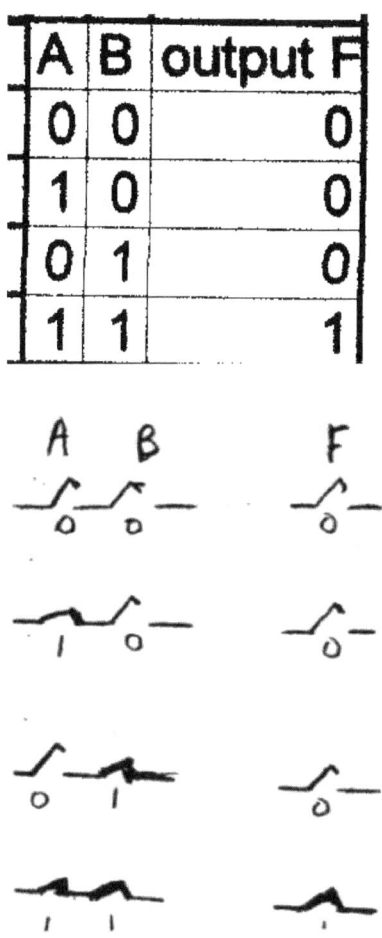

Gate Symbol:

Should the door was required to open if either A OR B were activated then OR gates would be used, as shown in the OR gate truth table:

OR Truth Table:

INPUT		OUTPUT
A	B	Function F
0	0	0
1	0	1
0	1	1
1	1	1

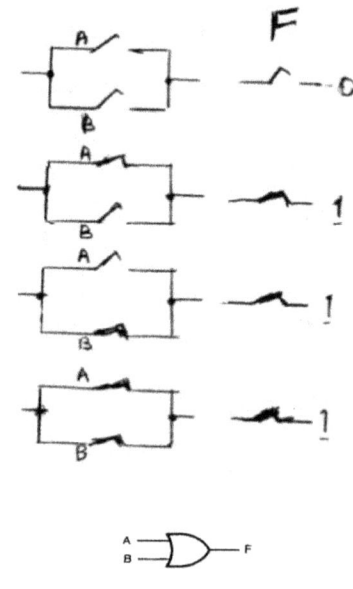

Other logic Truth tables, together with their Symbol

NOT (INVERT)

INPUT		OUTPUT	
A	B	Function F	
0			1
1			0

Symbol:

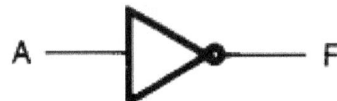

NAND (NOT AND)

INPUT		OUTPUT	
A	B	F	F
0	0		1
1	0		1
0	1		1
1	1		0

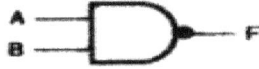

NOR (NOT OR)

INPUT		OUTPUT	
A	B		F
0	0		1
1	0		0
0	1		0
1	1		0

EXCLUSIVE OR, (A OR B,

INPUT		OUTPUT	
A	B	Function F	
0	0	0	
1	0	1	
0	1	1	
1	1	0	

But not both

100

A combination of these logic gates are used to perform programs such as the full adder below:

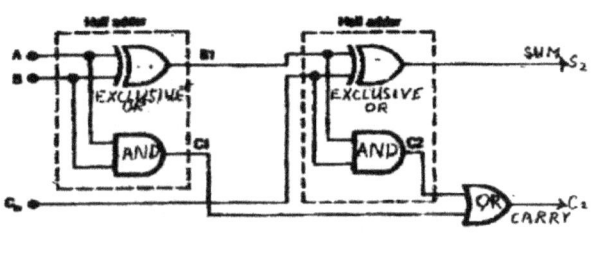

IN			OUT	
A	B	C	SUM	CARRY
0	0	0	0	0
0	0	1	1	0
0	1	0	1	0
0	1	1	0	1
1	0	0	1	0
1	0	1	0	1
1	1	0	0	1
1	1	1	1	1

The two half adders have truth tables of their own, but why complicate it?

Truth tables can also be defined as Boolean algebra equations. However the algebraic terms differ from those of conventional algebra. This chapter is to offer an explanation of the nature of "DIGITTAL," not to teach it, for which an appropriate textbook is recommended.

CHAPTER 9

James Clerk Maxwell 1831 - 1879

Enabler of the World Wide Web

At Cambridge in
1855 with his spinning red, blue and green disc.

Boole, De Morgan, and Babbage, were not the only great mathematicians of the nineteenth century to have a profound effect witnessed over a hundred year later during the post-war years. James Clerk Maxwell, probably the greatest physicist and mathematician of all prior to Einstein, formulated "Maxwell's Equations" to predict the transmission of electromagnetic waves. Could he have predicted their use to enable the World Wide Web?

He showed an interest in mathematics and science at an early age writing papers whilst still a student at Edinburgh University.

At Trinity College Cambridge he graduated as 2nd wrangler. Following a spell at Aberdeen as Professor of Mathematics he returned to Cambridge as the first Cavendish Professor of Physics, supervising the development of the Cavendish Laboratories.

During his early work on the nature of light he demonstrated by means of a spinning disk that any colour could be generated from three primary colours red, green and blue, the basis of colour Television a hundred years later.

Following further investigations Maxwell predicted the speed of light to be 300,000,000 metres per second, saying before the Royal Society of London in 1864:

"We have strong reason to conclude that light itself - including radiant heat, and other radiation, if any, is an electromagnetic disturbance in the form of waves propagated through the electromagnetic field obeying electro-magnetic laws."

Einstein, inspired by Maxwell's equations extended them further to formulate the theory of relativity, saying: "The special theory of relativity owes its origins to Maxwell's equations of the Electromagnetic field." - as does the World Wide Web!

The following poem composed by Professor Keith Moffatt in a celebration of Clerk Maxwell says it all:

When James Clerk Maxwell was a lad,
His questing mind fair deaved his Dad;
For "What's the go of it?" he'd speir,
An' hammer on till a' was clear.

They ca'd him 'dafty' at the scule,
An' that, ye'd think, was awfie cruel!
He didna' mind, he was apart
Constructing ovals o' Descartes!

He played wi' colours blue an' green
An' red, enhanced by glorious sheen;
An' took the earliest colour photo,
As good as ony Blake or Giotto.

He analyzed the rings o' Saturn,
Resolving their striated pattern,
Predicting weel their composition
By calculus and long division.

Redundant in the granite city
An' spurned by En'bro', mair's the pity,
He ended up awa' doon South,
Nae doot they thocht him gae uncouth!

He liked tae doodle lines o' force,
Wi' charge an' current as the source;

104

As much at hame wi' rho an phi,
An' E an' B an' J forbye!

Through these he dreamt up waves o' licht,
An' workit on them day an' nicht;
His mind roamed far whaur ithers durn't.
An' hit upon displacement current.

Syne back tae Galloway he repaired,
He had tae go — he was the laird!
By day conferring wi' the ghillie,
By nicht luc' brating willy-nilly.

At last frae Cambridge cam' the call,
Doon tae thon hallowed Senate Hall,
Where, tho' he held the dons in thrall,
They didna follow him at all!

Blithe son o' Gallovidian hills
O' birk-clad slopes an' tumbling rills,
Wha rose through intellect sublime,
Tae comprehend baith space an' time;

Great Scot! Wha's words in prose an ryme
Inspire us yet o'er vales o.time
In this thine eponymial year
Thy soaring spirit we revere.

CHAPTER 10

Hertz and Marconi

Link to the new era

Heinrich Hertz - 1857-1894

Maxwell's theoretical prediction of the transmission of waves through space was confirmed by Heinrich Hertz in 1886 using a spark gap to generate electromagnetic waves and a dipole similar to those used for the earliest television sets for both transmission and reception. It forms the basis of Wireless Technology, the greatest triumph of physics of the 19th century. However Hertz considered it to have no practical importance!

Whilst Heinrich Hertz's paternal antecedents were Jewish his maternal parents were Lutheran Christians and Hertz considered himself a Lutheran. Nevertheless Hitler had the commemorative picture of Hertz in Hamburg's City Hall removed. A memorial has since been set up at the Karlsruhe Institute of Technology, the site of his experiments.

Guglielmo Marconi 1874-1947

It was left to Guglielmo Marconi, experimenting at his father's estate in Italy to appreciate the possibilities of the wire-less transmission of Morse code. His work together with others, such as Sir Oliver Lodge, introducing channel tuning circuits, led to the establishment of world-wide radio; but this was Analogue Technology and, for the general public, a one way system, apart from licenced amateur radio "Hams," licenced to operate their own transmitters. But change was on the way, following the advances of technology witnessed during world-war II.

Marconi was of Italian/Irish parantage, born near Bolognia of an Irish mother in 1874. Studying physics at technical school he took an interest in the work of Hertz and Maxwell, starting to carry out experiments in 1894 at his father's estate in the bolognia region.

Like Hertz he used a spark discharger to generate electromagnetic waves. By connecting a vertical aerial rod to one end of a coil of wire connected to one end of the spark gap and a grounded metal plate at the other end he could detect the transmitted waves up to a distance of 1½ miles, enough to convince him that the transmission electromagnetic waves could provide a new method of communication. However receiving no encouragement in Italy for further work to exploit this possibility he travelled to London where he gave a demonstation of "wire-less" morse code to the chief engineer of the post office, Sir William Preece. Sir William immediately realising importance. in particular for communication throughout the British Empire, encouraged further work.

In 1897, back in Italy, Marconi established wireless telegraphy from a ground station to an Italian warship over a distance of 14 miles, encouraging him to set the Wireless Telegraph and Signals Company Ltd (later named Marconi Wireless Telegraph Company Ltd). In 1899 the company operating in conjunction with the British Navy exchanged messages between two battle ships over a ditance of 120 miles. This did not prevent scepticism among the scientific community who believed that this was the limit of the range as, like light, it would not be able to extend over the horizon - around 120 miles!

Undaunted Marconi continued to investigate the use of different wavelengths and in 1901 astounded the world by receiving the transmission of signals across the Atlantic, leading to the investigation of signal reflection by the the ionosphere by Appleton and others, including John Logie Baird.

Marconi was still active during the interwar years and is known to have met Baird on one occasion maintaining that he had no interest in television, his main interest being the "Skip Distance" of electromagnetic waves (now referred to as radio waves) over the horizon, bouncing off the upper atmosphere; nevertheless the Marconi Company did all they could to thwart Baird's effort to develop commercial television, eventually succeding when in 1939 they were chosen to broadcast television from the BBC transmitters.

Early spark gap transmissions prduced waves across a wide spectum of frequencies. This was overcome by th development of the "tuned circuit" enabling channel spacing of the transmission and reception of signal wavelengths over a defined frequency range. Although the first patent for this was taken out by Marconi in 1900, it was in fact the work of others, notably, Professor Sir Oliver Lodge of Birminham University and NikolaTesla in the USA. The Marconi patent was annulled in 1942.

The breakthrough from wireless telegraphy to wireless telephony was primarily due the invention of the themionic valve by J Ambrose Flemming and Lee De Forest which vastly improved the signal detection at the receiver and replaced the use of the crude spark gap at the transmitter to generate a cleaner and more powerful signal at the transmitter, enabling not only speech to be trnsmitted wirelessly but music as well. Public broardcasting began with the setting up of th British Broadcasting Company in 1922, followed by the the beugeonning radio industry.

Sir Oliver Lodge FRS 1851-1940

It is worth mentioning the important work of Sir Oiver Lodge. A friend and collaberator of Hertz he was transmitting and receiving electromagnetic waves a year prior to Marconi, using an iron-filings coherer for detection, a device consisting of a tube of iron filings that would cohere into straight lines in the presence of electromagnetic waves enbling them to become conductuctive and operate a buzzer (for instance). The coherer was invented by Edouard Bradly but improvd by Lodge, later to be used by Marconi.

Lodge, as an academic at Liverpool univesity at the time, was following up the work of Maxwell and Hertz, and although recognising the potential for the wire-less transmission of telegraphy took no part in its commercial exploitation. However he had many interests.

Born in Stoke-on Trent in 1851(then named Penkhull) he left school at the age of 14 to help in his father's business marketing all types of clay for the flourishng potteries. Whilst staying with his aunt in London he attended Lectures at London university wwhere he developed an enthusiasm for physics, with a special interest in the things that work secretly but had to be understood mentally.

He graduated at London University in in 1875 ,obtaining a doctorate in 1977, moving to University College Liverpool in 1881 He was appointed Principal of Birmingham University in 1900 and President of the British Association in 1913, retiring in 1920.

Although the most import contribution he made to wireless communication was the tuned circuit for channel spacing, he had a very wide range of other interests.

Like many scientists prior to Einstien he could not conceive of the transmission of energy such as electromagnetic energy, or indeed any sort of energy, without a medium through which to transmit it; generally referred to as aether. This was one of the imponderable things that work secretly that had intrigued Lodge as a student in the first place and intrigued him ever since He felt that the universe seemed a reservoir of life to which we really belong. However Einstein's Special Theory of Relativity published in 1903 made the idea of this medium redundant. Nonetheless Lodge held on to it for many years.

He could be very practical. He invented and patented the moving coil loudspeaker used in most radios today. He improved the design of early motor car sparking plugs which were later manufactured by Lodge plugs Ltd, formed by two of his sons..

Although not active in politics Lodge lectured together with Sidney Webb and George Bernard Shaw at the London School of Econmics.

Marconi as an entrepreneur had little interest as to whether electomagnetic waves travelled through a media or not, concerned mainly with extending the range of reception with a view to world-wide wireless telegraphy communication; an important link to the innovation of the International team of the Cern scientist's world wide web; an innovation led by

.an international team and made freely available internationally. A lesson here?

CHAPTER 11

Alan Turing, Thomas H Flowers, "FC" Williams

Creators of the digital era

The work of the four great Mathematicians of the nineteenth century remained in the closets of the academic world for a hundred years exploding into the public domain during the post-war years

Alan Turing - 1912-1954

Thomas H Flowers
1905 – 1998

"FC" Williams
1911 - 1977

Thus the work of the nineteenth century physicists, mathematicians and logicians lead directly to the beginning of the digital era one hundred years on, first appearing in Alan Turing's concept whilst at Cambridge in 1931 of a machine capable of computing "anything that was computable," later to be defined as a Turing Machine.

Turing's natural ability was noted early; yet despite this he was still keen to extend his education as widely as possible; to such an extent that when due to start the first day of term at a new independent public school in Sherborne coinciding with the general strike of 1926 he cycled the 60 miles from St Leonards-on Sea, stopping overnight at an inn, rather than miss a day's tuition.

He need not have bothered for the headmaster at Sherborne wrote to his parents: "I hope he will not fall between two stools. If he is to stay at a public school he must become educated. If he is to become solely a scientific specialist he is wasting his time at a public school." Apparently this did not deter him for at the age of 16 he had a comprehensive understanding of Einstein's equations.

The death of a friend At Sherborne turned Turing into an atheist believing all phenomena, including the working of the brain, were material.

Turing continued his education at Kings College Cambridge, gaining a first class honours degree in mathematics. At the age of 22 was elected a fellow at Kings on the basis of a dissertation.

From 1936 to 1938 he was studying at Princetown University in the USA where he was awarded a PhD for his dissertation on Systems of Logic based on Ordinals. During this time Turing was also working part time on cryptanalysis in conjunction with the government leading to his work in Hut 8 at Bletchley Park, of which it was said, "You needed genius at Bletchley; Turing was that genius."

His work at Bletchley Park during the war has been covered extensively elsewhere; however the building of the first operational Digital computer and his participation in its construction is sometimes misconstrued.

Following his work on the Bombe decryption machine Turing sought help to build a faster and more comprehensive system to decrypt the more complex Lorenz cypher Such help was forthcoming from "Tommy" Flowers, a senior engineer developing electronic switching telephone exchanges at the Post Office research establishment at Dollis Hill..

Turing was impressed with Flowers work recommending him to the team at Bletchley Park suggesting he should build the machine based on "Turing Machines.

There has been some misconception that it was Turing who actually built the Colossus. It was Flowers, on the recommendation of Turing, who developed it. The controversy related to Flowers recommendation of the use of thermionic valves rather than electro-magnetic devices for switching. This was opposed by the senior scientists at Bletchley Park, including Turing on the basis of reliability, particularly aggressively by Turing's fellow cryptanalyst Gordon Welchman calling it a waste of valves! However Flowers having had experience of the use of valves for telephone switching decided to go ahead at his own expense with the support of the head of the Post Office research centre at Dollis Hill. It was completed there in eleven months using no less than 1,500 thermionic valves.

Thus did the first electronic digital computer come into existence, mounted in several six foot post office racks. Its speed was a fraction of to-days laptops and several thousand times their size and weight. Nonetheless it was five times faster than could have been achieved with electro-mechanical switching. A second Colossus was built using 2,400 valves. A total of ten were built in all in the UK.

Thomas Flowers MBE was born in London's east end, the son of a bricklayer, in 1903' Whilst serving as an apprentice at the Royal Arsenal in Woolwich he attended evening classes at London University leading to a degree in electrical engineering and an appointment at the Post Office research labs at Dollis Hill.

Following his appointment to work on the Colossus with the code-breakers at Bletchley Park he returned to Dollis Hill. But unable to follow up this work due to the official secrets act he continued with the development of electronic telephone exchanges, also helping in the development of Ernie, the Premium Bonds computer.

In1964 he joined Standard Telephones and Cables Ltd as head of The Advanced Development Group Developing the System X telephone exchange at New Southgate, the same location as the author at that time, who lost one of his senior engineers to his group!

The UK lead in computer technology was squandered after the war as a result of knowledge gained at Bletchley not allowed in the public domain. However Alan Turing worked on the Automatic Computer Machine (ACE) at the National Physical Laboratory, a government organisation, where the details of his work was known, but there was little interest and only a pilot Ace computer was completed. Turing, frustrated, returned to Cambridge, writing a paper on Intelligent Machines and turned his attention to mathematical biology until his tragic death in 1952.

Professor Sir F C Williams FRS
Unlike Turing and Flowers "FC," as he was generally known, was not that well known to the general public; yet the importance of his contribution to computers and electronics in general scanned both the interwar and post-war period; linked by his vital contributions at the Telecommunication Research Establishment (TRE) during World-WAR II.

F C Williams studied Engineering at Manchester University gaining an MSc in 1933, and two years later following a College apprenticeship at the Metropolitan-Vickers engineering firm, went on to do two years research at Oxford university for which he was awarded a DPhil for his work on circuit and valve noise, after which he returned to Manchester University, where apart from lecturing, he published no less than twenty papers relating mainly to circuit theory. In 1936 he was awarded a DSc by the university at the comparatively early age of twenty eight.

His innovation of the operational amplifier, the use of thermionic valves for functions other than amplifiers and signal detectors, as in radio receivers, was vital to the more advanced development of radar, and subsequent development of analogue electronics prior to the introduction of digital circuits.

His reputation and extensive knowledge of circuit technology was known to Professor Blacket, a member of the Tizard Committee responsible for the setting up of the Air Ministry Research Establishment, the forerunner of TRE. Thus F C Williams was recruited to join Watson-Watt at Bawdsey Manor in 1939, where he made valuable contributions to IFF (Identification Friend or Foe?) later to be group leader of future development. He was also involved in AI (Airborne Interception) and the navigational aid code named Oboe.

This work was witnessed, or rather witnessed at arms-length, by the author whilst at the TRE, using circuits developed by FC; notably the variable time delay circuit he called the Phantastron, used to, simulate the delay between go-and-return pulses of radar for training equipment, the province of the author.

How was it that the author remembers hearing the many references to FC, whilst in no way involved with him on site? It was surely on the hockey pitch! For there was both a men's and mixed weekend hockey team for which, it is believed he may have played, possibly as captain; but it was a long time ago! The point is that despite being one of the elite boffins, unlike them his formal title was never or seldom heard. It was many years before the author new of it. Such was the man who masterminded the first digital computer to be produced for the open market.

Following the war, and following two years at the Radiation Laboratory in the United States where he contributed to their twenty four volume series on Electrical Engineering, FC returned again to his old University in Manchester. Appointed to the chair of Electro-techniques, he concentrating his research on digital memory storage. This culminated in the design of the Manchester Mark 1 digital computer, the basis of the Ferranti Mark1, the world's first commercially marketed digital computer.

During this post-war period of austerity the UK had maintained a lead in computer technology. Despite the economic recovery of the swinging sixties this lead was lost, just as the UK lead in radar was lost to the might of the United States market. IBM took the lead in main frame computers. Even so they depended on electronic memories initiated by the work of "FC" Williams.

Like De Morgan and others before him FC believed in the dissemination of knowledge and answered the disdain of arts academics of profits to scientists from patents with the comparison to royalties from books; Always a champion of the engineer asking "Why is it laudable and proper to show that a thing can be done, but improper to do it?"

The apparent end to lean times in the "sixties" turned out to be a delusion. Innovation had moved to Silicon Valley. In the UK financiers seemed to have taken over industry. One prominent financier is believed to have commented of his cash pile that leaving it in the bank was more profitable than investing it in industry; yet it was industrial innovation that had created the cash. It should have been put back into research and development, rather than being used to increase equity. Eventually the great GEC conglomerate died of R&D starvation!

CHAPTER 12

The Silicon Chip

\G W A Dummer OBE, 1909-2002,
the author's ex-boss.

So how did the era of the universal use of the
digital computer and associated Apps come
about? Although the Author did not directly take
any part of development of this digital

transformation, he was, nonetheless a witness to this dramatic and important change in technology enabling the digital era to flourish - the development the silicon semiconductor leading to the "Silicon Chip" was pivotal in the final breakthrough to the internet and World Wide Web

It was predicted by G W A Dummer the author's old boss at TRE.

Silicon, was initially used, together with a wire spring, for the detection of radio waves emanating the first of the BBC transmitters in the early the wireless sets of the 1920s; nicknamed the Cat's Whisker; but its importance was not recognised until the development of microwave radar during the second world-war when, due to its small dimensions, it was resurrected as a replacement for the diode valve.

It was reasonable to believe that just as the development of the diode valve by Ambrose Fleming in 1904 was followed by the development of the amplifying triode valve by Lee de Forest that the silicon semiconductor diode would be followed by a similar break through - and so it was.

Investigations into the nature of silicon were carried out by a team lead by William Shockley at the Bell Labs in America leading in 1948 to the development of the transistor. This was indeed analogous to the development of the triode thermionic valve four decades earlier, and replaced the valve in future radio receivers and similar low power electronic devices, triggering a surge in further research, not only in America, but across the world, in particular Japan and the Far-East.

In the UK G W A Dummer, initially group leader of the radar training group at TRE, was seconded to investigate the poor failure rate of electronic components in the field and continued to take an interest in component reliability in general post-war. He stated at an Electronic Components Symposium Washington In 1952:

"With the advent of the transistor and the work on semi-conductors generally, it now seems possible to envisage electronic equipment in a solid block with no connecting wires;" probably the first public description of an integrated circuit, *"for"* he went on, "a*s well as size reduction. I thought the only way we could ever attain our aim was in the form of a solid block. You then do away with all contact problems, and have a small circuit with high reliability. That is why I went on with it. I shook the industry to the bone. I was trying to make them realise how important it would be for the future of microelectronics and the economy.*

A pointer to the future?

Dummer was an idea's and committee man rather than a doer. As group leader he would allocate a project, but was not known for offering technical advice as to how to carry it out! Nonetheless he shouted loud and clear advocating integrated circuits.

He managed to arrange the placement of a contract with the Plessey company, which although strong in the manufacturing sector of electro-mechanical components such as automatic gramophone record changers, was not known for expertise in advanced research and development. Ferranti following from the successful development of the first marketable digital computer would have been ideal, or the cash rich GEC/Marconi group had the capability, but not the will to risk R & D, despite Dummer arranging a demonstration at the Royal Radar Establishment (formally TRE) in 1956.

Two years later Jack Kilby of Texas Instruments took out a patent for a similar arrangement! Had EMI of Hayes one of the largest manufacturers of radios in the UK at that time taken up Dummer's proposal there may have been a Silicon Valley adjacent to Heathrow Airport.

With the arrival of the silicon chip, the use of Boolean logic, Maxwell's equations, computers and satellites it is now possible to place billions of bits of data on a single chip and transfer it instantly across the globe.

There is a new world out there! Where will the new innovative breakthroughs using the acquired knowledge of past decades come from?

Will the importance of Knowledge Management as witnessed in the past be at last appreciated?

CHAPTER 13

Growth of the Management of Knowledge

Standard Telephones and Cables (STC)
management information meeting circa 1951, the
year that the author joined the establishment as a
junior engineer.

The emphasis so far has been a witness of
individual innovation. A different approach is
recommended for large and international
organisations. Innovate or die is the watchword.

Many organisations that have grown from
individual entrepreneurs and innovators are taken
up by professional managers, financiers, or
accountants, quite rightly when the organisation
grows beyond the capability of one individual.
Nevertheless stagnation is often the result. The

British motor industry as witnessed during the post-war years is an example of this. Why?

Capital is not only financial. "People are capital, holding intellectual capital (IC), as witnessed in the chapter on the growth of the Port of Felixstowe where little or no financial capital was available, and none was offered. The local work force using innovative procedures and flexible working practises outstripped the traditional inflexible ports to found the greatest container port in the UK, and one of the largest in the world. Furthermore the knowledge gained through the use of IC created knowledge that, carefully managed following transfer of ownership, enabled further successful operation and expansion.

"Knowledge is power" - John Bacon (1600). "Imagination is more important than knowledge" - Einstein. Combine the two, as witnessed in the chapter on John Logie Baird, who with only IC and helpful friends developed the successful transmission of public television ahead of the cash rich international players. In this case, following the formation of Baird Television Company, the acquired knowledge was not properly managed and Baird's lead in the broadcasting of television was lost to others. What does this tell us about corporate knowledge management?

The author was fortunate during the post war period to join a large international corporation and witness the successful management of knowledge across the mighty ITT (International Telephone and Telegraph), the British arm of which, Telephones and Cables (STC), employing up to 25,000 in the UK.

Although in the international field ITT may have been involved in some questionable political activities, in Chile for example, this had no relevance to the independent management of their satellite operations such as STC in the UK

Witnessing the operation of STC, with its international cooperation with ITT, illustrated a natural culture of knowledge management; leading to successful innovation.   ITT was referred by some wits as International Talk and Travelling;   indeed whilst only in middle management the author made many trips to ITT Federal Labs in New Jersey during the 1960s. This culture did not appear to be formalised and probably arose due to its roots being in Communications. However the culture can only be supported from the top, filtering down to all facets of the organisation.

STC Group 3750 shown below occupied three laboratories situated on a long passage together with perhaps seven or eight other labs, thus all the research and development covering several disciplines were in close touch. Furthermore they would be in touch with STL (Standard Telephone Laboratories), pure research labs in Harlow and ITT Federal Labs in the USA as necessary. This was a cultural rather than a formal arrangement for communicating with Labs across the organisation. For instance if the chief Engineer, at STC decided it was necessary to contact his counterpart in another part of the world then he would not hesitate to do it. Likewise individual engineers may be in informal contact with contemporaries in other countries. It was also helpful that the chief engineer, C E Strong, of long standing and high repute, who ran the New Southgate Radio Division until his retirement in 1965 knew the value of intellectual capital, setting up The STC Radio Society, meeting regularly to disseminate knowledge through the presentation of papers and discussions (tacit knowledge to explicit knowledge).

This free flow of knowledge is not always common throughout industry, and sometimes, as in the traditional docks post-war, innovation through new knowledge was actually discouraged. The result is witnessed in the chapter on the Port of Felixstowe.

Information management as witnessed by the author is not confined to the acquisition of data, important though it is. Knowledge falls into two different categories: tacit knowledge and explicit knowledge.

An example of tacit knowledge may best be explained by the authors own personal experience in the immediate post-war years, following tacit knowledge already gained among some of the country's leading academics at TRE:

On joining STC in 1949 as a junior engineer I was fortunate in being attached to John Birchenough (third left on the front row below – also ex-TRE) as his assistant. John was a graduate of Imperial College, London, considered at that time to one of the best engineering colleges in the world, consequently his knowledge extended well beyond electrical engineering; in depth knowledge across all engineering disciplines. Working alongside him for many years I acquired a wealth of tacit knowledge which was invaluable for the rest of my career, and, I hope, to others.

Explicit knowledge, as the word suggests, data that already exists; knowledge that can be captured, recorded and codified. Today there is a mass of data available on the internet, useless unless relevant to the matter in hand when it becomes Intelligence Capital. However it needs to be managed properly; it is an enabler in the acquisition and dissemination of knowledge.

Project Managers are beginning to appreciate the need for knowledge management, but the existence of yet another department in a large organisation, undoubtedly already clogged with excessive bureaucracy, may be not be such a good idea; better to generate a culture encouraged from the very top as witnessed at STC.

Group3750 of the STC Radio Division, New Southgate, with the author, second from right in the back row of the picture, soon after joining the division as a junior engineer in 1951. John Birchenough, his mentor, is sitting third from the right in the front row of the picture.

CHAPTER 14

Life before television!

Life was good before the advent of television, computers and supermarkets!

Radio was fairly new when the author was born in 1924; in fact he can remember the first wireless set (the name radio came later) to enter the home. It was an "Ormand" portable - portable in name only. Due to the lead-acid 2 volt accumulator needed to heat cathodes of the thermionic valves, the 120 volt high tension battery to power to power them, together with a smaller 9 volt "grid bias" battery, it could barely be lifted. However it caused great excitement at the time, but soon became boring; there were much more exciting things to do than sit listening to the radio, and the life of the batteries inhibited is use for background music until the advent of mains operated radios, not to mention the advent of pirate radio stations to play more popular music than the BBC, pity though about the adverts.

There were few cars on the road and virtually none outside houses in the streets leaving them safe for cyclists, not only for children to roam far and wide, but for parents as well. There may have been few cars outside the shops in the high streets of provincial towns but the pavements were lined with cycles parked along the sides of the roads supported by one pedal resting on the kerb. No special cycling clothes were used men simply attached a pair of cycle clips to the bottom of their trousers, or often as not tucked them into their socks; women, their bikes having no cross bar, simply slipped sideways onto the saddle and pedalled off.

Shopping was actually easier. There being no supermarkets the butcher, baker, grocer, greengrocer shoe-shop etc. all being within walking distance on the local high street, often closer than the length of the isles of large super markets, were easily accessible with no need to drive out of town with associated parking problems. There was no need to shop for a whole week at a time when it was possible and easy to walk or cycle to the local shops, - far more sociable, and, it was not necessary to search for what you wanted. You were served politely from the assistant behind the counter and did not fiddle with smart cards but simply paid the assistant with cash.

The bicycle really did play an important part of life. Almost every one, young and old, had a bike. This enabled a more efficient delivery by cycle than is available from the supermarkets by van. How could this be? It could not be with today's legislation for it would involve a young errand boy on his cycle. A phone call to the butcher, grocer or some such would result in an almost immediate delivery by bicycle peddled enthusiastically at maximum speed by a young lad, under age and underpaid by today's standard. Yes, it was right that the school leaving age should be raised. However this first work and earning experience is missing today. The youngsters were witnessed to be happier, leaner perhaps, than their counterparts of today riding their bikes "no hands" happily whistling the latest tune from Radio Luxemburg and laughing and joking with their friends as they passed. How often is whistling tunes in the street heard today?

Another great use of the bicycle, still seen today was by the postman, prior to 1939 happily delivering the penny post (240 pence to the pound pre-war) in time to be read at breakfast. It costs £1 for that privilege today and then it is only guaranteed before nine a.m!

A bottle of fresh milk would also be on the doorstep in time for breakfast, delivered at this period not by bicycle but by horse and cart; much more convenient for the milkman than a van; the horse would get to know the route and stops, walking alongside the milkman, stopping at each house as necessary. Between roads the milkman would jump up to the box and with a flip of the reins and a "giddy-up old gal/boy" trot off to his next location, maybe calling greetings to familiar passers-by.

Whilst milk would be delivered to virtually every household in time for breakfast, fresh bread was also an option, and what delicious bread it was, often still warm from the oven of the local baker, with a lovely crisp crust at each end, perfect for children with a thick layer of dripping saved from yesterday's roast! With few cars, and children invariably walking or cycling to school, even if their parents did own a car, problems of overweight and associated high cholesterol did not appear to be a problem.

The motor car, together with associated road transport, whilst convenient, was only "good in parts." To a large extent it damaged local communities, typically with the loss of local facilities and activities. This was particularly apparent in the immediate post war period. A typical example witnessed in the village of Trimley in Suffolk was that of the local Pork Butcher generally known as Porky Smith. People came from far and wide for his sausages, made from locally slaughtered pigs from the local pig farm, of which there were quite a few. Porky Smith is no longer there, but if a resident of Trimley, perhaps living in his original shop fancied sausages for lunch the pork may well originate from the local pig farm of which there are still many but it may well the pig would need to go by van or lorry to an approved abattoir, then maybe several more hundred miles to the preferred supplier of the local supermarket to be made into mass produced sausages, travel back to the Trimley or nearby supermarket to be picked up by car by the consumer living within cycling distance of the original pig.

Worse is a glass of water available from the kitchen tap, still an option today. However supermarkets have shelves full of bottled water. A very popular brand is transported by road and rail from southern France or Switzerland to supermarkets in the UK possibly as far as Northern Scotland. It is understood that Highland Spring from Scotland is popular in Southern France, so travelling the same distance in the opposite direction, polluting the atmosphere and making it as expensive, or more so, than the locally produced milk.

The rise of television ownership to the majority of the population by the 1960s coincided with events occurring at a time when the baby boomers of 1947 and beyond were youthful teenagers growing up into a society coming out of wartime and post war austerity, emerging at a time of prosperity, optimism and breakthroughs in technology not known by the previous generation. They seized this with enthusiasm. The 1960s belonged to youth as never before. This was manifest at a superficial level by pop groups such as the Beatles and others, but went far deeper.

The swift advance of technology beyond television, quickly absorbed by the burgeoning youthful generation, was confusing to the older conservative (small c) generation. This new youth had no time for the old concepts;, no patience with starting at the bottom and working

141

up to a higher level, but to leap-frog straight to high fliers. A widening generation gap was emerging. Young women were seeking independence, taking charge of their lives, living in pads of their own, taking executive occupations, and with the advent of "the pill" changing for ever a way of life, for good or bad, that would have been inconceivable a generation earlier. The speed of change and pace of life together with underlying anxieties of the cold war and the nuclear age was not without its adverse effects. "Stop the world I want to get off" was more than a light-hearted catch phrase; it mirrored a real anxiety. Some, mainly among the "have-nots," did indeed opt out taking to drugs, resulting in the alarming increase of drug addiction and consequent crime.

Whilst some young high fliers made it to the top there was also a burgeoning underclass that appeared to have missed out. Another gap was appearing, a gap between those that had it and those that hadn't. Whilst there were tragic periods of unemployment pre-war it was mainly amongst the adult population in the heavy industrial areas. Post-war traditional paths for youth such as apprenticeships, the armed forces or manual jobs were no longer readily available. Benefits eased the pain, but did not clear the problem. Again despair was a factor in the rise of drug addiction and crime.

The post war advance of science and the nature of the universe had a devastating effect on the place of religion in society. Church congregations shrank; Sunday schools in many churches disappeared altogether. The baby boom generation grew up with a greater knowledge of the development of the universe than any previous generation. This polarised conflict between the expanding universe and Genesis; an unnecessary conflict as it is generally considered that recorded history as far as the west was concerned did not begin before the tine of Abraham.

Nobel prize-winner in physics (1964), Charles Townes, known for his fundamental work leading to the development of the Laser, and astronomical investigations on the origin of the expanding universe, is also an active Christian, commenting in 1964: – "Science and Religion are much more parallel than most people think and in the long run must merge."

In Europe a new idea was taking shape, led be France and West Germany leading formation of the European Economic Community enshrined in the Treaty of Rome, signed in 1957 and taken into effect on the 1st of January 1958.

The UK was not part of the community at this time, although there was a continuing debate as to whether it should join for it was pointed out that the treaty was more comprehensive than a trade agreement. It contained the basis of a future political union with European law overriding national law, its founders believing with some justification that a unified Europe would make another catastrophic world war unlikely.

As early as 1964 the matter of sovereignty was clearly stated. In a case before the European Court, namely Costa v Enel, the Court stated that the Treaty of Rome "comes with it a permanent limitation of sovereign rights." Quoting from the community's publication The ABC of Community Law Dr Klaus-Dieter Borchardt, the author, states: "Firstly: the Member States have definitely transferred sovereign rights to a community created by them. They cannot reverse this process by means of subsequent unilateral measures inconsistent with the Community concept. Secondly: it is a principle of the treaty that no Member State may call into question the status of Community law as a system uniformly and generally applicable throughout the Community. It follows from this that Community law which was enacted in accordance with the powers laid down in the treaties, has priority over any conflicting law of the Member States. Not only is it stronger than earlier national law, but it also has a limiting effect on laws adopted subsequently."

The full extent of this loss of sovereignty was not fully appreciated by an island nation not at that time unduly interested about affairs going on across the channel. However there was considerable concern amongst those that had studied the extensive scope of the treaty, set in concrete and having no flexibility as an untried concept taking no account of politics of the future. Some, such as Enoch Powell, declaring it flawed and unlikely to succeed; were ridiculed and side-lined.

Others such as Earnest Bevin, an advocate of a united Europe before such a concept was any sort of proposition, speaking of the League of Nations in 1939, was prophetically aware of any cut and dried proposition saying:

*For years it has been my job to promote unity amongst conflicting organisations and **I would never have succeeded if I had put before them cut and dried constitutions.***

Even earlier Professor Heathcote Parkinson, author of the satirical publication Parkinson's Law wrote:

*Examples abound of new institutions coming into existence with an establishment of executives, consultants etc. in a building specially designed for their purpose. Experience proves that such a building will die. ...**It cannot grow naturally, for it is already grown**. When we see an example of such planning...the experts among us shake their heads sadly...and tiptoe quietly away.*

The EU continues to be a controversial issue.

One concludes.

With the coming of IT and consequent "people power" the landscape is undergoing fundamental changes. The new era is becoming far more complex than the old!

Conclusion

Examples of innovation in hard times indicate that when the economy is difficult corporations are reluctant spend money on research and development or innovative procedures, leading to further stagnation of the economy, and there are pressures to resist innovations which could increase efficiency that could mean an increase in unemployment in the short term. However both these short term attitudes delay economic recovery leading to increased unemployment in areas where innovation was discouraged as witnessed in the docks industry.

It is often against this negative trend that individual innovation has shown the way often against the odds.

Following the global economic collapse of 2008 there are popular institutional efforts to promote entrepreneurial innovation, welcome as this is, examples show that institutional and corporate activities can block personal initiative.

Comment by Malcolm Baird:

"The book's main purpose is to provide case studies (from actual experience) as opposed to an academic treatment (analysis)."

"The analysis of information is important, but it is tricky and not everyone agrees with a particular analysis. In that way it resembles the analysis of stock markets – not always 100% successful!"

"Looking back at my technical career, my research produced some data and some analysis. My feeling is that the DATA is more useful, in that it is still there to be built into later (improved) analysis in the future:" (*i.e. George Boole's 'Boolean logic' developed in the mid-1800s resurfacing for the Turing machines and internet nearly 200 years later, and Clerk Maxwell's equations later triggered Einstein's theory of relativity).*

"As Sherlock Holmes said, it is a capital mistake to theorise without data"!

"Another thought that comes to mind is that innovation is like fixing a roof, if the weather is fine you don't need it, if the weather is wet it is difficult to get the work done!"

END

www.ingramcontent.com/pod-product-compliance
Lightning Source LLC
Chambersburg PA
CBHW051919170526
45168CB00001B/462